DYNAMICS OF THE EMPOWERED SCHOOL: GETTING TO THE CORE

Joseph W. Hoff

Printed in the United States of America.

Please direct inquiries to:
Joseph W. Hoff
The E Factor
35 Kirklees Road
Pittsford, New York 14534

Cover design by Robert Mayo and PAM Grafix.

ISBN: 0-9636285-0-X

To Peggy
who encourages me to dream.

Table of Contents

Preface

Somewhere along the way we've forgotten how to work with one another. Somewhere along the way we've fallen prey to the finger pointing and rhetoric of failure. Perhaps the two are related.

Education, like managing a baseball team or decorating a house, is one of those things that people think they can do better than the experts. After all, everybody has been to school and has taught something to someone at one time or another. Everbody knows what school is and how it ought to be run.

Increasingly educators are getting "should" and "will" messages sent their way. "Schools should"..."test scores will"...and so on and so forth. Critics complain – theoreticians talk of restructuring – policy makers direct outcomes – and schools scramble.

TIME OUT! While I would be among the first to say that we haven't pressed our limits to the fullest extent, educators today are doing a very fine job under very difficult circumstances. But we can do better, and we need to do better.

Society has changed. So too have our kids. Resources and answers that may once have come easily are increasingly harder to obtain. Yet sad to say, schools have not confronted organizational growth to the degree that we must. We have neglected to ask ourselves a fundamental question, "Why are we doing what we're doing?"

DYNAMICS OF THE EMPOWERED SCHOOL: GETTING TO THE CORE addresses that question. It not only assesses the reasons why we do things in a certain fashion, but answers the crucial question, "What can we do to make our schools increasingly more successful?" The DYNAMICS discussed in these pages are critical to the development of an empowered organization. However, people who choose to make a difference, remains the most important ingredient.

Unlike those whose selective memory looks back to a "rosier" time, this work suggests a different tack. Its underlying premise is that we have *not as yet* come to grips with the potential inherent in our organizations. We have not yet gotten to the core of who we are, what we stand for, and how we can magnify the rich talent already present within our organizations. This book challenges all to do so.

GETTING TO THE CORE features stars. Unlike sports, entertainment, or the arts, education does not provide standing ovations for its people. Yet stars shine every day in our schools. The insights you receive are directly attributed to them, their talent, their joy in working with children and colleagues, and their willingness to grow and share. Being in their presence enriches me daily.

The stars to whom I am particularly indebted are many. I am grateful to John DeBaun, Julia Hahn, and Don Seidel for their encouragement especially during the early phases of my work. A new venture is as fragile as a butterfly's wing. Their support and gentle editing enabled my efforts to take flight.

To my mentors whose insights are woven throughout this tapestry I acknowledge Dennis Boike and Conrad Toepfer. Their inspiration, wisdom, friendship, and gentle push have helped me to create.

To Colleen Currie, Trish McCoy, Sara Pulver and Ken Huth I am deeply indebted. Their ability to capture what others cannot even see is a special gift; sincere thanks for sharing that creativity with others.

The old line..."I didn't have time to write a short essay so I wrote a long one," rings all too true. When genius has a wry wit, a breadth and clarity of experience, and a southern charm I think of John Lounsbury. His editing gave form and substance to my efforts. His perspective has sharpened my skilll as a writer just as his wisdom has helped me to grow through the years.

When kudos are handed out none are more deserved than those given to Barbara Johnson, Eileen Kelly and Sandy McCauley. Without their talented, ever pleasant support this project could never have been completed.

To my great children, Joe, Chris and Margery...thanks. Their encouragement and keen sense of humor have helped keep things in perspective. (Special thanks to Joe for the superb typing and computer graphics.)

My wonderful wife Peggy deserves a share of the credit for this work. Her balance, advice, encouragement and love have been a major source of reassurance. My resolve to go beyond the ordinary, to sail new waters is largely due to her confidence and support.

I stand and applaud all of these special people and the staff of Churchville-Chili Middle School. Somewhere along the way you discovered how to work with one another and in so doing serve as beacons to others. In giving to others you have modeled a commitment that places you among the finest of the very finest.

And to those who contemplate *GETTING TO THE CORE* by coming together and creating your own empowered organization I devote this powerful poem.

THE COLD WITHIN

Six humans trapped by happenstance
In black and bitter cold;
Each possessed a stick of wood,
Or so the story's told.

Their dying fire in need of logs,
The first woman held hers back,
For on the faces around the fire
She noticed one was black.

The next man looking cross the way
Saw one not of his church,
and couldn't bring himself to give
The fire his stick of birch.

The third one sat in tattered clothes,
He gave his coat a hitch.
Why should his log be put to use
To warm the idle rich?

The rich man just sat back and thought
Of the wealth he had in store,
And how to keep what he had earned
From the lazy, shiftless poor.

The black man's face bespoke revenge
As the fire passed from his sight.
For all he saw in his stick of wood
Was a chance to spite the white

And the last of this forlorn group
Did naught except for gain.
Giving only to those who gave
Was how he played the game.

The logs held tight in death's still hands
Was proof of human sin.
They didn't die from the cold without;
They died from the cold within.

Author Unknown

Introduction

The manner in which an organization responds to circumstances that differ from the norm often provides a look at the fundamental value system and quality of that organization. Just as humans react according to their perception, habit, need and emotion, organizational reactions run the gamut as well. This true story demonstrates how people who consciously choose to make a difference can create a positive organizational reaction from an unusual circumstance that directly affected one of its members.

Some people open their eyes well before the sun has risen with renewed vigor ready to face the challenges of the day to come. The principal wasn't one of them.

One particular morning his slumber continued well beyond the unheeded call of the 6:00 a.m. alarm.

Somehow he stirred...glanced at the clock and received a message that made him sit bolt upright in bed...6:55! He uttered something unprintable and proceeded to break the land speed record for completing his morning routine. Shaving while dressing he flew through the house, grabbed his shoes from a darkened closet, jumped into his car and sped to school.

"Pretty good," he thought as he arrived with two minutes to spare. Walking quickly through the parking lot he glanced down...only to find that he was wearing one brown and one black shoe.

What should he do? What would you do if you had to walk in his shoes that morning? After all, here was the PRINCIPAL – keeper of the kingdom; leader; one who sets the tone for the stability of the school; the rock upon whom others depend. Principals don't make mistakes – do they? His image and credibility were on the line.

This is what our hero did...

• He slowed his pace, raised his head and laughed hysterically!

• He then recalled a phrase attributed to Mark Twain:

When you're being tarred and feathered and ridden out of town on a rail, get out front and make it look like a parade!

Admiring Twain's wisdom, knowing that principals need to show their humanity, that they do indeed make mistakes, and recognizing that laughter is everybody's business, the principal decided to let others enjoy a good laugh at his expense. He quickened his pace.

• Possessing the biggest Cheshire Cat grin imaginable, into the office he bounded, pirouetting, moon-walking and exhorting everyone within range, (like the sneaker commercial) to..."Check out the shoes!" The dozen or so who witnessed this entrance promptly became laughing emissaries to those who hadn't been there.

• Now happenstance was on the principal's side that day for the school was celebrating Spirit week. Grabbing a number of spirit buttons he circled the line of his pant cuffs. The special tee-shirt with the school's mascot was broken out to complete the ensemble.

• Into the halls, just as Twain suggested, went the principal (like *The Music Man's* Robert Preston) out front leading the parade. The staff, kids, and the principal himself loved it – they all had a smile-filled day. The following morning bound and determined to wear his finest suit complemented by his best pair of *matching* shoes the principal arrived early to school. Smiling faces met his. There were more people than usual in the office. And when his eyes dropped he saw that his greeting committee had all worn dissimilar, unmatched shoes! As he was later to find, almost the entire staff had worn unmatched footwear to school. By the end of the day the students had picked up the theme and traded one shoe with friends so that the building reverberated with laughter and a delightful sense of spirit and unity.

Staff members followed the lead of the principal.

What actually happened in this true story illustrates the content of this book. We gain a measure of people through observation of the simple things they do. It has been said that we can learn more in watching a person in an hour of play than in one day of work. That is why examples drawn from actual school situations are heavily utilized in this volume. Vignettes that illustrate points made in the text will guide readers and increase their understanding.

When the principal felt the stress of too little time, his normal routine was broken and he made a mistake. (Perfectionism: Chapter 3.)

In discovering his unmatched shoes and deciding not to return home (a round trip of 40 miles) he faced a number of alternatives. Do I sneak into the office and hide my feet under the desk? Run to the store and buy another pair? Impose on a family member to bring me the correct match? Remove one shoe, bandage my foot and limp around all day (only to have a miraculous recovery tomorrow)?

You might have selected a different course of action. But the principal decided to "lean" on who he was, secure enough to demonstrate that substance is more important than image. He knew that though important, the *image* of the principalship is far less important than the *substance* of the person who occupies that role. (Leadership: Chapter 7.) His philosophic tendencies, in this situation influenced by a great writer (Twain) gave him clarity when indecision could have prevailed. (Learning Theory: Chapter 1.)

People quickly communicated the news of the day. They did so not to humiliate but to validate – and to live the fact that laughter is essential in an effective organization. (Communications: Chapters 1 and 7.)

The Latin phrase, *carpe diem,* SEIZE THE DAY, occurs naturally in the culture of an empowered organization. Teachers used the happening to seize teachable moments and captured them in their lessons, particularly in the expressive areas of writing and art. (Enabling Environment: Chapter 8.)

Students found that even a stated adult leader can make a mistake and that the security of the school was there to support that individual. A subtle but powerful message was thereby modeled. (Years of Growth: Years of Challenge: Chapter 2.)

When the staff demonstrated their unity by taking the initiative and rallying around a theme, they shared a common purpose and understanding. (Empowerment: Chapter 6.) Their culture encouraged people to laugh and enjoy one another in the place called school.

And when the principal dealt ineffectively with his choice of footwear, he demonstrated that, though well intentioned, the manner in which one faces change may have many unanticipated outcomes. (Change: Chapter 4.)

This volume will provide opportunities for you to highlight the feats of many; to tie both time tested and new interpretations of empowerment directly to the arena of school. The school that becomes effective consists of people who share the responsibility and vision that they have helped to create. The school that remains effective continues to create and continuously builds on its base of success.

I sincerely hope this effort will motivate you to confidently reach for uncommon success as you get to the core of your empowered organization.

Chapter 1

Learning Theory: It's a Matter of Triangles

How do you present a topic, that although fundamental, is typically viewed negatively? After considerable contemplation and the rejection of a number of approaches, I had a flash – at 2:00 a.m. Learning theory is a matter of triangles! Permit me to explain.

Heightened learning comes when there is intrinsic motivation, personal interest. As educators, we all know that fact. We also know that people can relate to simplified diagrams and symbols. Ad agencies have used this knowledge for years.

Of course, this is true only if they fall within the bare majority of adults who are able to think abstractly. One non-abstract thinker was asked *under which sign he was conceived*. Rather than providing a typical response such as Capricorn, Leo, Scorpio, etc., he replied, "Keep off the grass." Abstractions didn't quite make it with this individual.

Examples drawn from real life heighten our understanding and accelerate our connections to learning. This *connectedness* is what learning theory is all about.

The triangle is visually and symbolically connected. It conjures up notions of flow, one direction to another, to yet another. Learning theory deals with interrelated ideas possessing multiple intersections of dependent and reinforcing concepts. The triangle portrays a single dimension object that can pictorially hold other geometric shapes within its boundaries. Learning theory also contains a wide assortment of ideas within its framework. When triangles are balanced as in the equilateral variety, or used in conjunction with other triangles as in engineering, they become support mechanisms for other structures. In our case, the structure of the empowered school is supported by the values we possess through the foundations of our philosophical theories.

Fundamental learning theory also encourages the application of key concepts and leads to more intricate structures (thought). In simplified terms, both triangles and learning theory provide the base upon which complexities may be founded.

Is this logic circumspect? Let's take a look at some examples to see how ideas flow and triangulate into higher planes of practical thinking.

5

LEARNING TRIANGLE

Knowledge in and of itself gives the mature, reflective learner a sense of satisfaction and confidence. But what good are facts for the sake of facts? Let's face it, unless you are considering tropical manioc farming or plan to compete for the washer/dryer on a television quiz show, one *really* doesn't need to know the average precipitation in the rain forest of the Amazon Basin! Yet, there is a fundamental relationship of *knowledge* – even rain forest facts – to the *process of learning*.

A key concept educators need to address is the *linkage* that knowledge has to the creation of an independent/committed learner; one who applies learning to a course of action that might ultimately have a bearing on the quality of life and/or the human condition. Facts on the forest, linked to influencing mankind? Is this circumspect reasoning? Perhaps, yet perhaps not; read on.

William Purkey (1978) captures the essence of " linkages" in learning with his Learning Triangle.

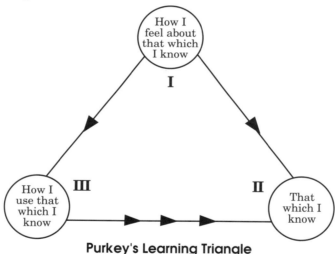

Purkey's Learning Triangle

As learners, if we are to own knowledge then we must be *confident* in our ability to apply that knowledge to a life situation or course of action. The teacher who presents, reinforces, and models knowledge (concepts) in such a way as to instill confidence in the learner's actual or perceived ability (learning self-esteem) increases the probability that the knowledge will be effectively retained and later applied by the learner. Application reinforces the learning and completes Purkey's loop. It looks like this:

"That which I know" (KNOWLEDGE), leads to
"How I feel about that which I know" (CONFIDENCE), and
"How I use that which I know" (APPLICATION).

The Learning Triangle permits one to gain clear and powerful insights about the linkages within the process of learning.

The teacher's role has increased importance as we apply Purkey's theory. The presentation of material, scheduling of reinforcement activities, and engagement and encouragement of the student, depend to a major degree on the skills of the teacher. The attitudes that the teachers model and their personal commitment to the utilization of knowledge increases the probability that students will confidently apply their own learning. An instructional unit that requires rote memorization and little engagement of students inhibits learning. Enlightened teachers are aware of these barriers and engage the students in learning through both activities and their personal example.

Thinking of the rain forest, the teacher who utilizes group project activities such as letters to Congress on the depletion of acres of trees in that region establishes interdisciplinary lessons with team colleagues, and directly models a deep commitment to the environment through actions as well as words, influences the learners' confidence in their choices regarding "How to *Use* That Which I Know."

Henry Adams oft-cited belief, *Teachers affect eternity, they can never tell where their influence stops,* is inherent in this logic. Students possessed with confidence in their learning (perhaps as a result of their understanding of what happens in the Amazon Basin) will help determine the fragile balance and future of our water planet. The Learning Triangle helps educators to develop that linkage.

HIERARCHY OF NEEDS

Social psychologist, Abraham H. Maslow, wrote extensively in the 40's and 50's of his studies of "adequate" personalities. Maslow pointed out that such persons had lives characterized by peak experiences, periods of time where people lived life to the hilt. Peaks (both momentary and prolonged) occur when people see broadly, feel intensely, communicate deeply, or respond completely. Maslow contends that the more people are able to have these kinds of experiences, the more self-realized, more adequate and stronger they become (1970).

In school or college many of us were too busy enjoying peak moments or seeking them to *reflectively assess* them for what they were or what they might have been. We didn't utilize Maslow's work to gain clearer insights about ourselves and our studies.

Interestingly enough many of the free spirits in an organization might find that this triangle has renewed meaning and substance. What many didn't utilize then could have significant personal and professional meaning for them now.

Maslow's students have designed a triangle based on his teachings. To ascend to a higher level requires the attainment of the lower level. The bottom levels are what psychologists refer to as deficiency levels. Unfortunately, more and more of our students are functioning at these stages. The homeless children rooted in unfulfilled PHYSICAL NEEDS (food, water, shelter and warmth) cannot attain the next level, SECURITY and SAFETY. And individuals who do not feel secure or safe cannot attain the next level; and so on. While we are justifiably occupied with concerns at the deficiency levels, we need to closely study the total triangle and especially concentrate on the location of KNOWL-EDGE and UNDERSTANDING.

If, as postulated by Maslow, higher needs are attained only when previous levels are fulfilled, then the implications for the educator are multiple.

Maslow's Hierarchy of Needs

Just as the hungry, cold child does not feel secure and safe, KNOWLEDGE AND UNDERSTANDING are not achieved, much less optimized, unless the child has a sense of LOVE/ BELONGING and/or feels worthwhile and valued (RESPECT/SELF-ESTEEM). Often we have heard instructors when asked what they teach, indicate the NAME OF THE COURSE! Fundamentally we all teach children. And what we teach children, in terms of our *attitude* and *nurturance*, determines to a major degree what content they will learn in our courses. A more thorough response to the aforementioned inquiry might have been – "I teach 7th grade children, social studies, language arts, and a whole lot more!" And you know we really do.

The effective school recognizes that security of belonging is essential to the students' development of confidence and connectedness to learning.

Research by Robert Allers (1982) suggests that children in pain who do not first turn to their parents *want* to seek out teachers 75% of the time. Unfortunately, only 25% do. Apparently while the school is viewed by students as a place of stability, a security net during personal times of turmoil, *only if educators invite them* will students reach out for assistance. Our choice is obvious.

Students at-risk of school failure often come from families that are dysfunctional. In the school, small nurturing units, academic teams, clusters, or clubs enhance belonging. While not able to replace the family, the organization's design of belonging (affiliation) is essential in enabling the learning to progress through the hierarchy in the world of school.

Picture the perfectionistic, eighth grade girl who has been a strong "A" student her entire school life. The child will now often set aside her academic emphasis to seek the love/belonging, and approval of friends. The sensitive teacher or counselor when aware of this drive is better able to provide the guidance that will result in the student's rapprochement with her internal conflict. The student is therefore encouraged to meet success on *both* an academic and social level. The enlightened professional does not ask what's wrong, but understands what is happening in the adolescent's life even when the child herself may not, will not, or cannot verbalize it. The ability to refocus the student to achieve higher levels of functioning is directly within the influence of the teacher.

Validated, secure students perform more effectively. The environment of the school and its classrooms is closely related to pupil success.

A nurturing environment in both individual classrooms and the school assists the attainment of a sense of worth, esteem, and belonging in the learner. The learning environment bridges the middle stages in the needs triangle to KNOWLEDGE/UNDERSTANDING and ultimately to the peak of fulfillment that Maslow presented in his fully actualized person (BEAUTY/SELF ACTUALIZATION). Knowledgeable empathic teachers design this linkage. In fact, self-esteem studies indicate that students undergoing the personal changes of adolescence value as significant those teachers who:

- Listen to students (take the time)

- Assign work that students do well (provide incremental success opportunities for their kids)

- Ask about students' outside interests (value the individual)

Johnston (1991) provides a slightly different slant to this theme when discussing the traits middle school students identify in their favorite teachers. He reports that adolescents value those who:

- Talk about us when we're not there (connectedness)

- Show up when they don't have to (care)

- Start conversations with us (communicate)

Powerful in its simplicity and validity – validity that is based on a sense of belonging.

As in Purkey's Learning Triangle, our second triangle depends on linkages. In Maslow's case, ascending variables, each a platform for further accomplishment, are critical to success. The elements of Maslow's self-actualized person and an interpretation of them warrant further comments. The self-actualized person has three basic qualities; seeing broadly, feeling intensely, and responding completely.

SEEING BROADLY depends in part on one's desire to be open to ideas and experiences. Independent, life-long learning occurs when the individual seeks and confidently applies learning skills. In order to see broadly, one must desire to do so. Successful learning experiences increase the desire for more. For example, in Purkey's triangle, confidence in one's learning enables the student to *apply* that learning – which leads to deeper, fuller knowledge – and to an attitude of life-long learning.

All people have feelings. Philosophers suggest FEELING INTENSELY occurs when people, as a result of being in touch with themselves, have a connectedness to the reasons why actions occur. Not that all feelings or actions must be truly understood. For example, a sense of joy doesn't need to be analyzed to be more fully enjoyed. Maslow contends that being in touch with essential information heightens the intensity of one's feeling. Heightened internal feelings increase the possibility of achieving peak experiences.

Communicating deeply elevates the success of everyone. One tongue-in-cheek definition of a school implies that "it is a loose collection of classrooms held together by a common parking lot." Many schools are like this quip. In those schools, we are all in this – alone. Unfortunately, many school people have traditionally viewed their interaction in schools in a negative light. Words like *trust, involvement, we / they* become terms that fragment rather than unify. We need to be connected to common goals through effective communications.

To be able to RESPOND COMPLETELY depends on one's confidence level and willingness to risk. Both factors depend on a strong sense of self. A positive sense of *self* is an essential component of both Purkey and Maslow's TRI-ANGLES. The school and the quality of its teaching process have a sizable impact on the individual's attainment of the highest levels on the *Hierarchy of Needs*. Maslow's insights are powerfully stated and symbolically captured on our second learning triangle.

LEARNING PYRAMID

One other triangle that warrants notice is the Learning Pyramid developed by Edgar Dale of Ohio State (*Building a Learning Environment*, 1972) and popularized by the National Training Laboratories of Bethel, Maine. It presents validated evidence dating back to the 1890's that *how we instruct* has a significant impact on the degree that students retain learning.

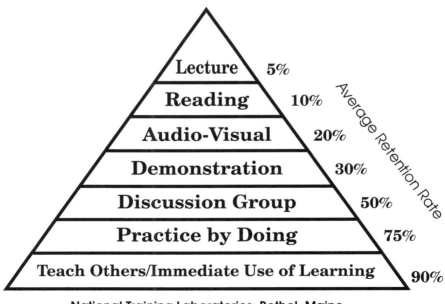

National Training Laboratories: Bethel, Maine

Learning Pyramid

Maslow's triangle visually scaled attainment upward to reach the fully actualized individual. The learning pyramid does the reverse. In this case bedrock foundations are created when learners apply their learning and teach others. An old saying goes:

Those who can, do. Those who can't, teach.

In light of the LEARNING PYRAMID, a more accurate phrase might be:

Those who can, do. And, those who teach, really know their material well!

Though educators intellectually embrace this philosophy, parallel data suggests that the format of talking at and calling upon students (lecture/recitation) comprises a significant amount of our instructional interaction with students. One would think that if teachers know that in teaching others student learning is reinforced, then the great preponderance of the interactions in our school settings would have pupils teach and immediately apply their learning. Unfortunately this isn't the typical case.

What percentage of the instructional time does lecture/recitation comprise at the secondary level? 50%? No, higher. 70%? No, higher. 85%? No, higher still! The *typical* secondary instructional style of lecture/recitation occurs as much as 95% of the time. (Buzan, 1983)

The intermediate elementary teacher (grades 4-6) says with a smile, "Not us, that doesn't pertain to us." Correct, say the data, intermediate teachers use lecture/recitation as their primary instructional mode only 88% of the time.

Surprising to you? Only primary teachers use this teaching procedure less than 50% of the time. We all need to be more *facilitators of learning* rather than *dispensers* of knowledge. Dale's study clearly confirms this point.

It doesn't take a Rhodes scholar to deduce from the PYRAMID that the more engaged the learner is in processing the desired learning, the higher the degree of retention. The more passive, the lower the rate of retention. Simple? Yes, but the fact is that we don't mix our instructional practices to the degree that we should. Call it conditioning, call it perennialism, call it comfort level, or whatever, the evidence is clear – our students are too passive and are not as engaged in their learning as they need to be. When students have been shadowed during a full school day, the resulting records reveal many things. Lounsbury's (1991) analysis of twenty-five years of shadow studies indicates that:

1. The school day as presently operated is both physically demanding and psychologically wearing.
2. Pupils, although well-behaved, are too passive.
3. Meaningful interaction between student and teacher is minimal.
4. The textbook dominates the instructional program.
5. The instructional program is fragmented, compartmentalized, and artificially removed from life.

Thanks to the work of Roger and David Johnson (1984), Robert Slavin (1983), and Carol Cummings (1983) alternatives to passive instruction are gaining prominence. *Collaborative learning* is more than a catch phrase and promise. It provides a framework for interactions that combine group and individual accountability. It also provides multiple opportunities for students to apply their learning by instructing/sharing with others. The teacher is still the conductor of the orchestra in blending the process of learning, but both knowledge dissemination and classroom interaction are dramatically enhanced when students are engaged in the process of their learning. To a major degree, teachers who are engaged in active instruction are more productive and feel better about their contributions to students. With the knowledge of the LEARNING PYRAMID and the confidence that comes from analysis and instructional success, the teacher can design and apply instructional strategies that increase engaged learning and retention.

But just as in collaborative learning where the whole is greater than the sum of its parts, we as adults and as contributors to our organizations must have a connectedness. Magnifying our talents (synergy) in an empowered organization results in a 1 + 1 = 3 equation because in our definition of TEAM...

Together
Everyone
Achieves
More!

How do we reach TEAM? How do we define synergy as one person plus another equalling three? How do we connect personally and professionally with our colleagues? This quest leads to our final triangle – the COMMUNICATIONS MOUNTAIN.

A maxim that through the years has had particular meaning for me is:

People don't trip over mountains,
They stumble over molehills!

R. L. Sharpe's inspiring poem, *A Bag of Tools* has parallel significance to the above maxim:

A Bag of Tools

*Isn't it strange
That Princes and Kings,
and clowns that caper
In sawdust rings,
and common people
Like you and me
Are builders for eternity?*

*To each is given a bag of tools,
A shapeless mass,
A book of rules;
And each must make –
Ere life has flown –
A **stumbling block**,
Or a **stepping stone**.*

This poem really hits home. Here's why.

Patterns predominate in our schools. What has been, more often than not, continues to be. Queries as to *why*, likely are answered by the response, "We've always done it that way." Minor problems or past hurts are clung to tightly, often at the expense of progress or an enhanced understanding of our colleagues.

Yet choice is possible. As in Sharpe's poem, we can choose to build an enabling structure or one that retards our progress. Conscious CHOICE is what creating empowered schools is all about!

In any organization, key people influence others. They fashion their organizational role, style, and communications to have a significant influence on the quality, openness, and ability to confront change that their organization needs to remain vibrant. *Key people have a key influence in shaping schools.*

We need to increase the number of key people in every organization – until everyone believes and lives that belief. Highlighting postively the value of all to the organization implements that philosophy. Here's an example.

I was asked to do a workshop for administrators on "Working with *Difficult* People." I refused. The series was renamed and I was able to conduct a workshop entitled "Working with *Different* People." Changing one word represented a substantial shift in emphasis. Words can be stumbling blocks or stepping stones. Communicating the success of everyone builds a momentum that is hard to deny.

Each of us can and should be a key player in empowering our organizations. We consciously choose whether we will trip over molehills or climb the heights. The altitude we reach depends on our attitude. In a real sense each of us has something unique and special to contribute. If you don't believe you'll make a difference, you won't. Thankfully, the converse is also true. *If you believe you can make a difference, you will!*

Dennis Boike(1992) shared the following idea with me.

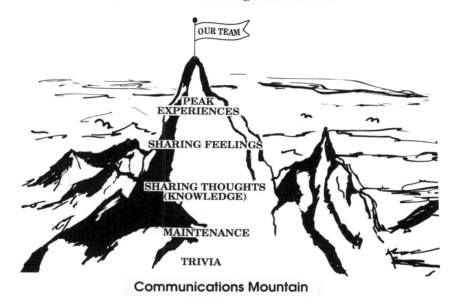

Communications Mountain

As with Maslow's Needs Hierarchy, our COMMUNICATIONS MOUNTAIN has as its summit, peak experiences. As with Maslow's fully actualized person, peaks are achieved when people see broadly, feel intensely, respond completely and communicate deeply.

How often do we provide opportunities to peak in our organizational communications? As German theologian Paul Tillich suggested, we seldom reach those communcation peaks where we transend our roles or patterns of superficial interaction and connect with others in a significant fashion. An "at-one-ment" occurs when two individuals are so bridged that they come together in deep understanding. As students learn key concepts in our classrooms, lightbulbs of awareness click on. When that happens teachers feel a real sense of accomplishment. An ovation spontaneously given by students or colleagues as a validation for you on a job well done are like hundreds of lightbulbs being turned on simultaneously and connect many in a peak experience. External affirmation through communications heightens peak experiences which are ultimately experienced within. Reaching new understandings with a significant other as a result of moments or ideas shared does that as well. The visit of a former student who had done much to turn your hair prematurely gray, but returns several years later with his child, to thank you, is a peak experience. He tells you now what he couldn't tell you then, what you meant to him during his conflicted time in junior high. As educators we all have examples we can isolate and retrieve. Some are deep inside, some near the surface. All are cherished.

Why, then, do so many schools present stumbling blocks? They do so because of habits, inability to break out of old patterns, the persistence of stereotypical thinking, and unwillingness to risk. It is time for a change. But how?

Developing effective communications is a positive first step. However, we don't begin that process by sharing our innermost feelings in a full staff meeting. Your comfort level isn't ready for that approach yet. If you do reveal all, your colleagues might patiently listen but flee for the exits when the meeting ends. Were you to do so, your administrator would gasp and move on to the next agenda item – reading a flawlessly typed discourse on the excessive use of the copy machine. We do not initially pour out our souls...time and readiness are essential.

We begin with assessing how our communications process operates. This knowledge may not necessarily tell us *what to do*, but an analysis of *what is* will point out what we should *not* do and what practices we should retain. For example, one might ask...Does this principal read memoranda at the bi-monthly staff meeting because of a fear of having the staff discuss key topics? Does the staff development program consist of a few attending a conference every third year only to have them keep any new insights to themselves? Is there a weekly bulletin issued from a central source that shares information about upcoming events, agenda, curriculum bits, professional opportunities, recognition of staff honors, etc.? Or does the mailbox flood with items at the seeming whim of the principal, often on the day before the activity is to occur or the form is due? *Assessing the existing patterns will enable an organization to deal with what it can become.*

Knowledge about the COMMUNICATIONS MOUNTAIN can be quite helpful also. Though a casual review might tempt one to denigrate the base level, TRIVIA, the reality is that all organizations need to have human interest communications. "How about those _____!" (insert your favorite regional sports team here) is necessary dialogue because it often connects people on safe levels. Safe communications augment the confidence that ultimately enables people to climb higher on the mountain toward a peak experience. The security of relating to people whom you know is essential to communications that can make a long-term difference.

However, there is an unwritten compact when you operate on the TRIVIA level. Teasing is appropriate...heaviness is not as this illustration demonstrates.

A colleague passing in the hall says to me, "How are you, Joe?" Were I to respond candidly I might say, "My house is a mess. Peg's redoing the kitchen. I've got to take out a major loan. I banged my ankle playing basketball last week and because it's raining outside it hurts like crazy. And besides the neighbor's mongrel, a Heinz 57 pooch, somehow had a clandestine meeting with my pedigree princess, Fifi, and she's..."

Subjected to that onslaught, the skin of my colleague will crawl and she'll flee to the sanctuary of her classroom. What the unwritten compact calls for to a "How are you?" greeting is a simple response like "Great!" as we smile and walk by one another on the way to fulfilling our separate agendas.

The TRIVIA level in our organization enables us to connect as people. Linkages based on interests and personalities, enable us to appreciate the substance of our colleagues. The TRIVIA level helps us to achieve a familiarity – a superficial understanding of who we are and what we value as people.

Communication targeted to MAINTENANCE is a component of an empowered school. Maintenance is the level that keeps the boat afloat. It is comprised of the procedures, routines, and information that are necessary to operate the organization. What time does the meeting start? When is the paperwork due? What are the pay dates? What's the background information on my new students? Organizational details are grounded in the MAINTENANCE level of our communications. Our organizational *inter*dependence requires a known structure within which we can operate securely.

When an organization fails to achieve satisfactory maintenance, the levels above are rarely realized. Details, short term and long range considerations, and a facilitative attitude on the part of the office are important factors in increasing the security of the staff. From a psychological perspective the more secure the individual, the more that individual can risk. One can share more in an organization or with people who are a part of an enabling structure. When schools fail to solve maintenance issues, the sharing of progress insights stops. In a dysfunctional setting, complaining predominates. Maintenance, then, is essential to organizational health.

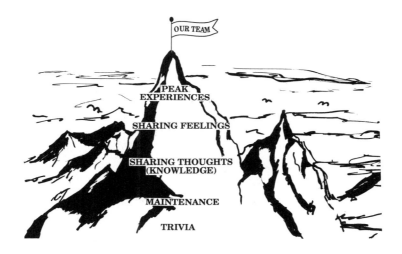

As we climb our mountain, let's concentrate on the next level, SHARING THOUGHTS. We reach this level to varying degrees in every organization. The key question is do we share information as much as we should? Ideas on instructional strategies, insights gained at a recent conference attended, pre- and post-parent conference data usually get shared, although typically not beyond the limited circle of grade level, department or team colleagues. The problem with "connecting" just a few individuals is that their separateness can create a negative valence within the organization. The resultant tension is often counter-productive to the realization of common goals. If the assessment suggested earlier reveals a pattern of bi-monthly staff sessions, in which an individual (or a few individuals) talk *at* not *with*, an "I-don't-wanna-be-here-but-I-gotta-be here" staff, then what *we* do about that reality becomes a key task. If the meeting design is flawed, then a whole host of creative alternatives may be considered.

Without being in your mocassins, it would be presumptive to suggest the absolute manner in which your school should come to grips with its organizational potential. For illustrative purposes, one scenario could involve a representative committee brainstorming possibilities for improvement as a preliminary to the total staff doing so in small group sessions. The caution is not to give in to the Nay Sayers who no doubt will indicate that, "This won't work; they won't let us... etc." When referring to negative people, keep in mind the witticism that they should:

LEAD...
    FOLLOW...
        or
          GET OUT OF THE WAY!

Alternatives that will engage people in the development of their organizations are needed. People do need to lead and/or support. Communication in an empowered school can consist of stumbling blocks...or stepping stones. People do indeed choose.

When the new principal joined the team at Churchville-Chili in 1985 there was a significant need to address a format change in communications and how meetings were conducted. Small group sessions as a portion of the all *staff* (note: not *faculty*) meetings became the *modus operandi*. Topics such as – *What can we do to improve our building's aesthetics? What are the impediments to learning that we have unconsciously built into our system and how do we change them?* and *How do we work more effectively with at-risk pupils?* became pro-active discussion topics.

When the right questions are asked, they are answered. When answers become calls to action, then results come in batches. When a large number of issues are effectively addressed, the school improves. This clarity of focus enabled meetings to become more productive. Positive communications increased the effectiveness of the total group.

A teacher leader who had served as an officer in the professional association was asked to compare Year #1 and Year #5 in terms of communications and results. The discussion went like this.

Interviewer: "Do you remember what you called those who tried to block the progress of the group in the first year of our efforts?"

Teacher/Leader: Somewhat sheepishly he replied, "Yes, I do...The Crabbies!"

Interviewer: "Do you remember how many 'crabbies' we had the first year?"

Teacher/Leader: "Approximately 25." (out of a total staff of 54)

Inteviewer: "In your best guess, how many do we have five years later?'

Teacher/Leader: He paused as if mentally reviewing the roster of staff and said, "About 2 or 3." (out of 75)

The formerly disconnected "crabs" are still on staff. Their positive focus and ownership of the organization's successes have helped them to grow and modifiy their previous blocking pattern.

What were some of the changes that helped transform staff communications? One meeting each year was devoted to "Bring 'n Brag" in which each staff member took a few minutes to share an idea, instructional technique, inspirational reading, or practical suggestion.

The music staff Loree Hartzler, Kevin Mead, Carol Pitkin and Mark Wheaton performing Kevin's composition, "I've Got the Bring'n Brag Blues".

In another, all staff took an in-building field trip. Staff met together for five minutes at the beginning of the session, grabbed a cup of coffee, teamed up with a few colleagues, and visited *every* classroom and *office* in the building.

Prior to leaving each room, the visitors wrote at least one positive comment about something good they had observed in the room. Talk about breaking down the walls of isolationism! Talk about recognizing the worth of every person! Talk about connectedness! This technique worked because it linked staff to the collective talent and common mission they all shared – instructing children. The meeting's design was positive, and so were the results.

```
              Staff In-School Field Trip

               Thursday, December 7

Teacher's Name ___Parnell_____

Room Number _____121_____

Comments from Colleagues:
```

Like your signs

WOW!!

Good scientific environment.

I like your atoms!

GREAT STORAGE AREAS

Great effort!

nice models.

Great room! Looks like fun!

Great Displays!!

Have you seen the can opener?

```
   Please tape this to a student desk closest to the door
   just prior to Thursday's meeting at 2:30.
```

When you share knowledge, gain increased confidence in your collective ability, and apply your knowledge (e.g.: through techniques such as "Bring'n Brag" or your in-building field trip) you increase the potential for improving collaboration. In essence, you build stepping stones. Though communications are used to connect people and maintain your organization's structure, people *share* operational information and establish new patterns that contribute to common understanding. When this happens you can reach the next plateau on your climb, SHARING FEELINGS.

When Joe was previously asked, "How are you?" he erred and actually told his colleague of the kitchen remodeling, his leg problem, and Fifi's impending motherhood. The place and timing were wrong. He misread the situation. Yet, when feelings are to be *effectively shared*, trust, understanding, and a common bond are necessary. When many of the "Crabbies" in Year #1 of our TEAM BUILDING process confronted any deviation in the pattern to which they had long been accustomed, they initially resisted it. Good, bad or indifferent, they resisted it. They wanted control over the variables of their lives. Today these same individuals are regarded as pro-active contributors to the momentum of the organization because their questions help to clarify procedures and the focus of our creativity. Those individuals are valued for the strength of their contributions and uniqueness. And, as a group, they no longer attempt to block progress.

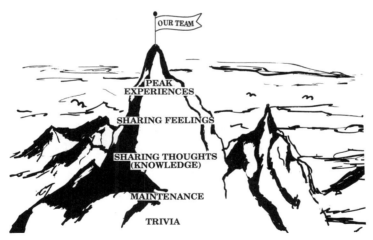

When professional contributions are valued, as are the individuals who make them, *feelings can be shared*. Timing is still essential. The forum is still critical. And the selection of the person(s) with whom to share is still a highly important personal choice. Share we can, share we will, and share we must. But how do we reach PEAK EXPERIENCES?

When we personally define heights of peak communication there is a blend of "centeredness" and "connection." They are the goals which we seek in further validating ourselves, both personally and professionally. We achieve them in our relationships with others.

Peak experiences are rare. They shine like jewels when we experience them. My colleagues and I have treasured them in the place we call school. I have reveled in them all.

When it was suggested that we have our initial "Bring'n Brag" session in lieu of the traditional "talk at you" staff meeting, fears of grievance action, massive absenteeism and the like predominated. We had the meeting. It went quite well. We post-mortemed our initial effort with an eye toward how we could make it even better.

The next year when we faced the meeting again it wasn't without apprehension (public speaking is the second greatest fear of adults, even teachers). Two staff members showed up for the sessions dressed in referee's outfits.

The self-appointed referee with watch and whistle insures that teachers don't go overtime in bragging.

Equipped with air horns and whistles they were the tongue-in-cheek "guardians" of the "2 minute" time limit. We laughed with tears of joy at these two wonderful characters whose antics helped us to transcend the fears of the moment. Five years later, although our refs have yet to whistle anyone who has gone beyond the limit, a sense of unity and fellowship has developed. We now print a booklet of our ideas and openly discuss the items we share.

For me, being a part of a process that confronted the effectiveness of our communications, a process that had succeeded in uncommon terms, was a peak experience. So you see, the feelings and information we share in school enables us to define who we are and how effective we can become. Pushing our limits or tempting the next level on the COMMUNICATIONS MOUNTAIN creates an attitude of questing – which results in individual and organizational growth. We aspire to the top, but must climb one step at a time.

SUMMARY

And so it is with our triangles. Learning Theory has meaning when we confidently apply it to reach new levels of success in our instruction. Learning Theory has applicability beyond "deficiency" when we truly understand and reach out to the children we teach. Learning Theory when orchestrated by professionals who are in touch with the need for a variety of teaching strategies unleashes the potential of individuals and groups. And Learning Theory inspires synergy when we connect as never before through open, focused peak communications (Communications Mountain). Learning Theory is a prime stepping stone to professional growth and organizational fulfillment. Learning Theory is the cornerstone of empowered schools. To paraphrase Henry David Thoreau...

> *If people advance confidently*
> *In the direction of dreams...*
> *They will meet*
> *With an uncommon success.*

Inspiring every child we teach and influencing colleagues to do so is our magnificent obsession. Having this high calling is critical to the achievement of an empowered school. Triangular logic will enable each of us to find uncommon success in achieving new heights of excellence. Challenging old assumptions from a secure base of understanding will assist in this quest. 🍎

Inspiring each student to reach for success is inherent in effective teaching.

Chapter 2

Years of Growth – Years of Challenge

According to research...

*80% of all first grade students have
high feelings of self-esteem
20% of all fifth graders have high
feelings of self-esteem
5% of all high school juniors have
high feelings of self-esteem*

– Jack Canfield, 1988

Have you ever worked with kindergarten students? They are a delight. Ask the little ones how many can sing. All hands shoot up. Ask them to sing. All do.

Ask them how many can draw – once more to a person they indicate they can. What can you draw? *Anything, wanna see? How about a tiger in a space suit riding on top of a garbage truck in front of your school? Okay, how big?* And a few minutes later that's what you'll have.

Ask those same questions of our middle schoolers. Can you sing? Can you draw? What will their responses be? First, they'll try to figure out what you're after. Then they will look around to see if anyone else is revealing their abilities – then they will go along with the majority. Ask them to sing or draw a tiger wearing a space suit riding on top of a garbage truck and what will you get? Some pretty contorted faces – some sneers, and possibly outright defiance, and little or no participation.

What a shame. The spontaneity, child-like wonder and joy of the kindergarteners have been submerged below the surface or lost altogether. Learners must have both an inner sense of self-confidence and trust in the individual asking those questions before they will risk an answer. The younger ones seem to have both – in bunches.

As we move along the continuum of schooling, what happens when high school or college students are asked if they can sing or draw? They will deny their abilities indicating that they haven't done anything like that since elementary school. Or they'll be too embarrassed to display their talents in front of their classmates. How sad. The spontaneity of our 5 year olds to the mistrust of 13 year olds to the alibiing defensiveness of young adults. What happened? What went wrong?

Mark Scharenbroich tells a delightful story which begins to answer these questions (*The Greatest Days of Your Life...so far*: A Jostens' Film Presentation). The type of behavior that is found in a controlling rather than enabling environment has a strong link to peer pressure and conformist behavior.

Ever observe in a first grade classroom? Think of the teacher asking a question of the class. All hands go up. The hands are raised as high as they can go. They're on their tip toes while sort of sitting down. They are busting at the seams to answer. They're wiggling, twisting, "ooh, ooh, oohing" and the like. They all want to be the one picked to answer.

The teacher is perplexed. "Now whom do I call on? Peggy, Johnnie, Katie, or Mark! Okay Mark, what's the answer?"

"Oh, oh...um, um...well...ah...dinosaurs!"

"Oh...Honey...we're talking about numbers today...but bless your heart for trying."

Meanwhile what's happening? The class is giggling and whispering..."Mark is dumb – ha, ha! – Mark is dumb!"

Mark looks around the room, hears what is being said, and starts to hold back a little to protect himself.

Let's go into a third grade class. About forty percent of the class raise their hands.

Seventh grade – about twenty percent. And those who do have their hands raised at half-mast. Most avoid eye contact with the teacher.

Tenth grade – a handful. Their hands? At half-mast. The rest stare at their desks.

Seniors – the teacher asks..."Anyone know the answer?" No hands. "Oh come on, someone, anyone! Please..."

By the time they are seniors the students' actions say..."Hey man – there's no way I'm going to put my hand in the air. Once burned, twice shy. I've played this game too many times."

And every time a teacher asks the kids a question, to share the gift of knowledge, the first thing the kids do is to stare at the tops of their desks. They have learned that to maintain eye contact with that teacher might increase their chances of getting called on.

The Road Not Taken

Two roads diverged in a yellow wood,
And sorry I could not travel both
And be one traveler, long I stood
And looked down one as far as I could
To where it bent in the undergrowth:

I shall be telling this with a sigh
Somewhere ages and ages hence:
Two roads diverged in a wood, and I –
I took the one less traveled by,
And that has made all the difference.

– Robert Frost

The empowered school understands its students just as an effective organization knows and understands its clientele. Whether choosing the road "less traveled by" as in Frost's classic poem or following the well-worn path, the school's goal must remain as "making all the diffference" for its students – the Marks, Marias and rainbow of names and backgrounds who seek the gift of knowledge.

In American schools we celebrate diversity.

They have been conditioned, as was little Mark, that to risk being right is not worth the humiliation of being wrong. Although an obvious exaggeration, Scharenbroich's story is a powerful one – one that illustrates how student initiative can be damaged through both peer ridicule and the teacher's inability to engage and develop the learner's contributions and sense of worth.

Ours is no easy task. Our ultimate success is not measured as much by the success of those motivated stars who let us shine in their light as it is by the success of the most challenging students, who are in their most conflicted period of development.

This chapter is devoted to an understanding of what arguably is the most difficult time of life, a time labelled by G. Stanley Hall as one of "storm and stress." The children in the middle level years; the crucial time known as EARLY ADOLESCENCE.

If we anticipate what follows our initial efforts in the elementary school, better provide for children during the bridging years, and build on the levels which preceed high school, the choices we make will benefit all throughout the K-12 journey through our schools. Knowledge and sensitivity will help us to choose the appropriate path for our children.

Reprinted with special permission of King Features Syndicate, Inc.

As Canfield reports and Scharenbroich portrays, we cannot accept the decline of student self-worth as absolute. We can and must construct the future. And as Hagar reminds us, we must constantly build for our successes.

A number of years ago I was facing a major decision. I wasn't certain to which level on our K-12 continuum I'd devote 65% of my conscious hours as an aspiring administrator. The words of a sage veteran helped me to decide.

> *If you want to be loved,*
> *   choose elementary school!*
> *If you want to be respected,*
> *   choose high school!*
> *If you want to be needed,*
> *   choose middle school!*

So, twenty years ago, I made the personal decision that I needed to be needed and chose to work with young adolescent learners. I haven't looked back once.

That doesn't mean that there haven't been times that "tried my soul," times when events dimmed the remembrance of happier grade levels long gone by. There have been moments when I would have gladly traded places with lion tamer, Gunter Gabel Williams; and would have worried if *he* were up to the task!

Yet effective middle grades educators need to possess an inner sense of security, a clarity of focus, a sense of mission, and an enduring joy. These traits enable one to weather difficult moments in dealing with the tempestuous yet delightful middle grades years of growth.

The ability to be calm in the eye of that storm comes once again from knowledge. Knowing that our adolescents' delicious honesty, blatant insecurity, raw curiousity, constant yearning, and open nerve endings, represent in total, a mere passage in time. Knowing that who they are and more importantly what they can become depends to a major degree on *us*. Knowing that these young- sters are on the staging ground of their adulthood. And knowing that we can and do make a difference in influencing the quality of their lives.

UNDERSTANDING ADOLESCENTS: AN OVERVIEW

If human development is a continuous process across the life span, what is adolescence? One wag wrote that "adolescence is a dynamic time of life that comes in with a pimple and goes out with a beard." An elementary colleague said "adolescence is that time between 11 and 18, when parents age 20 years." By its very nature we know that adolescence ultimately does end – it merely seems endless to parents who experence it, children who live it, and those of us who observe and teach it.

Adolescence is viewed primarily as a period of **physical development**, al- though it is much more. The Latin verb, *adolescere*, means to grow into maturity; and although their personal biological clocks are set to different time zones, they ultimately reach the maturity of adulthood. Adolescence, then, is the time of passage from childhood to adulthood.

Adolescence is also a sociological phenomenon. In the 1920's, G. Stanley Hall defined a female teenager as a "flapper" – one who vainly tries to fly while her wings only have pin feathers. Physical development is as old as the human race, although **social adolescence** is largely identifiable with Western culture. This view (without the rites of passage indigenous to more "primitive" cultures) says that despite his physical maturity, the adolescent remains a child. Our society does not accord him full adult status, function, role and responsibility.

In Western culture we prolong a child's dependency. In fact, the United States is argued to have the longest period of adolescence; in many cases extending well into the early twenties! Our kids today remain "flappers" for a long time. Their pin feathers are often imposed by familial, school, and societal systems that won't let go.

Adolescence has also been defined as an **age span**. While varying widely for individuals, and having differing onset periods for boys and girls, for the sake of our discussion let's narrow the range of adolescence to three phases:

Early Phase –	10-14 years old
Middle Phase –	15-16 years old
Late Phase –	17-20 years old

Psychological thinking varies as to the timing of the different phases. It doesn't much matter exactly what years are ascribed. What does matter is that there are discernible phases and that individual adolescents will engage them at different times and move through them at varying rates. To a major degree it "all comes out in the wash." Due to societal and nutritional influence, adolescence is manifesting itself earlier. Whereas adolescence may once have been viewed as a type of apprenticeship, few rites of passage exist today. The benchmark driver's license is one of the few that remains. Laws protect this age prerogative.

A religious ceremony such as a confirmation or bar mitzvah is a symbolic manifestation of "passing" from childhood to adulthood. Yet today this passage is rarely marked by full independence or by the acquisition of the responsibilities of an adult. In our society a youngster begins to be conscious about designer jeans at 6 1/2 years of age. Childhood and adult roles are confused. The future isn't what it used to be and one doesn't need to wonder what this reality has done to the stability of our kids.

So, adolescence may be defined as a stage of physical development, as a sociocultural phenomenon, as a discreet stage in development, and as a state of mind typical of individuals who are no longer children but not yet adults. All are valid aspects of adolescence.

ADOLESCENCE THROUGH THE YEARS

A trap into which we might unconsciously fall is to decry the present adolescent with righteous indignation and outright horror. As the hairs on our head turn gray, our memory becomes more selective. Three dramatic insights will provide an historical perspective.

> *The children now love luxury; they show disrespect for elders and love chatter in place of exercise. Children are tyrants, not the servants of their households. They no longer rise when their elders enter the room. They contradict their parents, chatter before company, gobble up daintees at the table, cross their legs, and tyrannize over their teachers.*

Know who penned this one? It was Socrates in ancient Greece, approximately 400 B.C. While it might be expressed a bit differently in your locale, you no doubt can relate readily to his view of adolescence.

Can you guess the author of this opinion of adolescence?

I would there were no age twixt ten and three and twenty, or that youth would sleep out the rest; for there is nothing in the between but getting wenches with child, wronging the ancientry, stealing and fighting.

If your choice was William Shakespeare, go to the head of the class.

Drawing from Shakespeare's logic, in our urban centers, crime is rampant and many adolescents become modern day street urchins. If today is an average day in our civilized society, then there are *40 fourteen year old girls* having not their first, not their second, but their third child! These are not just the urban poor. The data are drawn from every segment of our culture, urban, rural and suburban. Frightening? Yes. But the statistics are real.

D. Silliman Ives comes closer to our era when in the 1920's he wrote...

For the last ten years I have been a close observer of what has passed among the rising generation in this great metropolis (New York), and I cannot suppress the humiliating conviction that even pagan Rome, in the corrupt age of Augustus, never witnessed among certain classes of the young a more utter disregard of honor, of truth and piety, and even the commonest decencies of life.

So much for the good old days. Some additional sayings give further definition to this analysis.

An ancient Chinese curse is said to carry a terrible doom:

May you live in a time of transition.

That saying is clipped from the preface of a textbook on labor negotiations law, yet it has special applicability to adolescents. For they, too, are in a time of transition. Aside from fetal development, the life cycle undergoes no more rapid changes than in adolescence.

Were Booth Tarkington to write *SEVENTEEN* again he'd name it *ELEVEN*. This perspective is right on target. Generally speaking, Great Grandma matured as a woman at 17 years of age and great great grandchild, Margery, will get there somewhere between her eleventh and twelfth year. Boys in general do lag behind physically (16-24 months) but face accelerated expectations for their masculinity. Lay the social pressures on the youngster of the advertising ideal that they observe on the television, or view in their magazines, and you have a dramatically revised perspective for Booth Tarkington's original title.

As kids face challenges and go through phases, so too do their parents. There are three stages in life someone has said.

1. *My daddy can whip your daddy.*
2. *Aw, Dad, you don't know anything.*
3. *My father used to say.*

Two other sayings provide additional perspective.

The struggle of adolescence is the struggle within the child...dependence vs. independence. As parents, our need is to be needed. As teenagers theirs is not to be needed.

The sum of all these comments is that patience and understanding are key elements in the survival kit all parents need to have while their children experience these years of testing and trauma.

When the Eriksonian framework of adolescent tasks is reviewed later, more definition of the internal struggle alluded to in these sayings will be provided. The reality of the adolescent's struggle lies within. The "feel good" to a young child who is being cuddled and nurtured, is replaced by a desire for detachment from parents in the middle grades years. The parent who still wants to treat his teenage baby as a child has difficulty understanding this sudden change. The conflict in adolescence, like that ancient Chinese curse, is that adolescents are in the throes of transition. And parents who treat in-between-agers as either dependent or independent are destined to be wrong no matter which way they go.

Kids test their wings within secure structures. Assuming the family is secure, then dependence/independence issues become appropriate forums for anti-dependent behavior. Those youngsters who fail to press their limits (challenge/test) often have suppressed their ability to grow through the trial and error decision making process. Perfect little children run the risk of landing on the psychologist's couch at 35 years of age with developmental gaps in their personality formation.

In-between-agers need to press their limits. A nurturing structure with a consistent framework of known expectations and an open, validating regard for the child, are essential whether at home or in school. Balance and the right touch are highly necessary when dealing with youngsters who are conflicted with the natural process of establishing who they are in relation to issues of dependence/independence.

That right touch was described by Cervantes' classic character, Don Quixote de la Mancha, when this master fencer was asked how he held his sabre. Said Quixote...

I liken holding my sword were I to hold a dove. Not too firmly as to crush it, not too loosely as to have it fly away.

In more contemporary terms, one might describe an effective discipline strategy as:

Providing clear expectations to our students is essential. In fact, working with your kids is like holding a wet bar of soap. Too firmly and it shoots out of your hand...too loosely and it slips to the floor.

And while adults concern themselves with clarity and balance, adolescents are experiencing identity formation and personal change.

It is frightening to grow up...but it is humiliating to be little.

During this anxious time of transition, adolescents need a nurturing, consistent and well-defined structure to provide stability to their lives.

The child is father of the man.

The above line from an 1806 poem by William Wordsworth, "My Heart Leaps Up" is particularly poignant. As we recognize that the child is on the "staging ground of adulthood," the child is, indeed, father of the man or mother of the woman.

Not to deny the earlier assessments, the age of adolescence is also a time of opportunity. Properly handled, the challenge of working with adolescents is alive with positive energy. Our youngsters are a joy not only to behold, but to involve in the quest of discovery. Unleashing the inherent beauty of their "becoming" depends on us. Opportunity is there; knowledgeable teachers who nurture, guide and motivate, reach these vulnerable youth and inspire them to reach for the stars.

How the child emerges from the romantic stage of adolescence is how the subsequent life will be molded by ideals and colored by imagination.

– Alfred North Whitehead

Do we provide opportunities for our students to create...to dream...to help them define the ideals to which they can aspire? To write them off as flakes, unmotivated or dysfunctional is criminal. We often are the spark that lights the candle of their illumination. As educators we must live this mission.

Adolescence is a time for vision, self-discovery, sounding one's personal depth and potential, and feeling the pull of life.

Narrow, restrictive instruction produces single dimensional learning. Teachers then are likely to occupy their energies with **control** issues. Issues other than school curricula occupy the thoughts of students. We need to ask ourselves whether we are adequately engaging students in a dynamic enterprise in our classrooms. Given the controlling structure of so many classrooms and schools, how often do we focus our students' vision, encourage their connectedness to learning about life, or provide incremental successes which help them to answer the conflicts inherent in them as they feel the pull of life? To do these things regularly would dramatically increase our success and their learning.

People validate people. As educators, our role in working with adolescent learners, as Nancy Doda suggests, is to *think big* but *work small*. Having a sense of mission helps us to influence the success that students will ultimately achieve.

> *Ideals are like stars; you will not succeed in touching them with your hands. But like the seafaring man on the desert of waters, you choose them as your guides, and following them you will reach your destiny.*
>
> *– Carl Schurz*

STAGES OF DEVELOPMENT

One of the most insightful writers on adolescence is Erik Erikson (1968). His theories have been heavily utilized in this section.

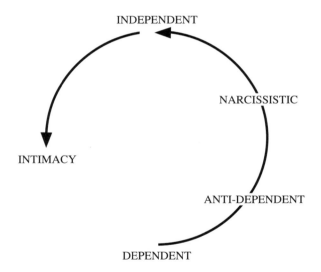

Psychologists interpret human development as a continuum of stages that occur throughout the life cycle. While only 38-40% of all adults reach the stage of INTIMACY, all but a few people eventually attain the capacity to become INDEPENDENT. The following insights might be helpful in better understanding that adolescence as in the Whitney Houston song title, is but *One Moment In Time.*

The first stage of life commences as we enter the world at birth. Every child starts out life with basic anxieties about survival. The attentive parent contains that stress by making the infant feel loved and secure. The newborn is DEPENDENT on its parents for sustenance, warmth, and loving responsiveness. Within the first four to six weeks the infant has learned to manipulate its environment to get what it desires – a knack many children never lose.

Moving from dependency to autonomy is one of the exigencies of life. To illustrate, picture the youngster who joins his parents on the weekly grocery shopping trip. How does the little one usually get around? Correct – by riding in the fold down seat of the shopping cart. That lasts for a while until the youngster gets antsy and ends up being given a box of animal crackers. The cookies enable the adults to get through the remainder of their serpentine movement through the aisles with minimal distraction. The little one rides, observes, and learns that goodies are contained in those multi-colored packages on the shelves.

Some time after mobility has been mastered, the child, no longer content to ride, walks through the store holding his parent's hand. He spies the animal crackers...lets go of the hand...moves to the shelf...turns to see if his parent is still there...then returns to the cart carrying the box.

In letting go the child basically tested his wings. In doing so, he checked to see if his security factor (the parent) was still present. He then completed the task. The child may then return to the comfortable perch on the cart happily eating giraffes, panthers, alligators and gorillas. Momentary independence has been successfully tested in a setting that is familiar, comfortable, and secure.

This visual example identifies the process of *detaching oneself* not from the nurturance of the parent, but from the direct control (hand holding) of the parent. The inherent psychological task for each human is ever thus – **to move from dependence to independence.**

In testing his wings on the way to the cookie shelf, the child's backward glance was taken to verify **trust**. On the next visit to the store, the glance may not be taken because security/trust was previously present. The elements of trust and security are necessary in positively developing the child's independence.

If the parent hadn't let go, if the parent created a tension that discouraged the child's initiative, or if the parent had reprimanded the youngster, the **trust** and **security** of new initiatives would not have been present. The child's confidence in moving toward a higher sense of autonomy would have been impeded.

It is not that parental neglect on a trip to the grocery store creates dysfunction in the development of a child's independence. The example merely illustrates how parents unconsciously enhance the development of trust in children. Denying trust engenders mistrust. And when dysfunctional patterns are deeply rooted, they are extremely difficult to unearth.

Age appropriate patterns of development are important especially in identifying dysfunctional students. The following age appropriate patterns illustrate what attainment/non-attainment creates.

Patterns

	If you don't develop these	*You develop these*
1-2 years	Trust	Distrust
2-3 years	Autonomy (Independence)	Shame, self-doubt
3-5 years	Initiative	Guilt
6-11 years	Industry	Inadequacy
11-30	Identity	Identity confusion

If children are constantly criticized for tasks they have initiated, they will not develop the desire to test new situations (risk). If meaningful tasks are not provided as a natural pattern of the family (or classroom) responsibility, then industriousness is not nurtured and feelings of self-doubt and inadequacy predominate.

Control is a strong motivator for parents and teachers alike. Many adults consciously limit the variables they have to contend with in order to succeed with the few they select. Adolescents are having many new variables thrown their way. They are simultaneously experiencing a highly introspective process – Who am I? What was I? Who might I become? That is why in the crucible of the adolescent years, children need to become ANTI-DEPENDENT!

Adolescents need to test their wings.

Adolescents naturally *test limits* without consciously determining to do so. When those limits are imposed by people who desire to CONTROL, the inevitable conflict of flint striking stone creates sparks.

If we understand the chemistry of this process, then school personnel can effectively guide students through this crucial period of human development. But we must view challenge as the natural testing or flapping of adolescent wings rather than as attempts to undermine our authority.

Just as family tasks completed by children in their formative years enhance feelings of adequacy and industriousness, decisions made by students, and their accountability for those decisions are important to adolescents' *identity* formation.

Of course we don't turn adolescents loose to do whatever the mood strikes them to do. Schools need to provide a structure of nurturance where...

> **limits are established**
> **limits are reasonable**
> **limits are clear**
> **limits are consistently presented and enforced.**

Having poorly defined limits can create dysfunction. Adolescents need to know the parameters within which they are able to operate. In the *anti-dependent* phase, they will press against these limits to know how far they can go.

Skinner's experiments with laboratory rats offer some clear insights on adolescent development. One experiment measured contentedness and dysfunction in these rodents. Three groups were established. Each was previously trained to push a special lever to obtain food pellets.

Group #1 received food pellets every time they pressed the lever. ***They were the best adjusted.***

Group #2 got no food pellets whenever they pressed the lever. ***They were the second best adjusted group.***

Group #3 was erratically reinforced. Sometimes they received food pellets. Sometimes they did not. ***They were in turmoil.***

These animals became so dysfunctional that they rubbed the skin off their snouts from constantly pressing the lever. Their dysfuntion came from unclear boundaries and inconsistent rewards. Let's move from the lab to the school setting.

Visitors to Churchville's 950 pupil middle school often comment on the responsiveness of the students and the warmth of the teaching/learning environment. They ask why this is so. The underlying principles that guide this success are simple, yet strong.

- Everyone counts
- Everyone makes a difference
- Privileges are earned
- You are responsible for your decisions
- Each is a contributor to the group
- Positive incentives are clearly identified and consistently presented so that clear *choices* are possible.

The school structure is an *enabling one* and will be discussed fully in Chapter 8.

In their time of anti-dependence, *choice* and the resultant responsibility adolescents have for the choices they make are essential. Do we provide a framework for choice in the controlling environment of school? Research and experience indicates not to the degree that we should! Yet dealing with the consequences of choice is how growth takes place.

Readers who are parents can no doubt relate to this scenario. *Anti-dependent* children are prone to test limits, especially in the evening when adult patience wears particularly thin. After an adolescent's unsuccessful negotiations to grab 15 additional minutes of we're-still-up-time, the parent may lose it and punctuate the still night air with...

Go to bed, and,

GO TO SLEEP!!!

Step back and analyze that gentle suggestion. Yes, it is possible to direct kids to go to bed; but I've never heard of anyone who has been able to mandate *sleep*. An enabling structure defines parameters and permits the individual to choose. This situation *might* be effectively framed:
Parent to a teenager:

> *In our house when your family jobs are done, you've completed your studies/homework, and we've found time to speak with one another as a family, you will have earned the right to choose what specific time between 9:30-10:30 p.m. that you will go to bed. Now, going to bed in our house means...there is no music playing, the Walkman's batteries are retired for the night, the lights are out, and the flashlight is not under the covers as you read your book...and if you so choose, YOU MAY STARE AT THE DARK CEILING ALL NIGHT!*

No one can *mandate sleep*. But we do define parameters. Within parameters responsibilities necessary to earn the right to choose (when to go to bed) may be established.

Choice within parameters – limits and incentives clearly established within a structure (perhaps mutually negotiated) enables each to respect the identity and decision making capabilities of the other(s). This framework needs to be applied to our schools and classrooms as well.

Choice and the process that one undergoes in choosing are powerful governors to the anti-dependent phase of development. We must provide choice opportunities to students in the school setting, all the while encouraging positive decisions relating to academics, group responsibility, and active participation in activities that benefit individuals, groups and the school itself. Valuing the individual at all times, yet reacting (approving/disapproving) to the decision the student has made, enhances the youngsters' development in that they have power in the formula. They create outcomes.

Perhaps you have seen the television spot of the child racing home with a straight "A" report card clutched firmly in hand. She races into the house – inadvertently slamming the screen door – consequently disturbing the sanctity of the home. Father, greatly disturbed, verbally attacks the adolescent. "What are you, stupid?   How dare you slam the door. Haven't you any sense...etc, etc."

The closing scene is of the father victoriously returning to the couch as the child quietly drops the report card into the garbage can. The image tears me apart.

Decisions are open for dialogue. Yet we must *never, never* invalidate the worth of the individual. We must unconditionally value the child – not invalidate the youngster if the door slams loudly. The action may be questionable – the person is not.

EARNING PRIVILEGES

In utilizing that line of reasoning, a cafeteria program that is a "whip and chair" operation does little to provide incentives for individual and group responsibility. Assigning seats and requiring kids to sit quietly, creates a tension that bubbles over to the hall and class(es) that follow the mid-day repast. Pouring what kids want, what they need, and what the situation requires into a blender can create a cafeteria mix with a different slant. It could look like this...

Structuring an Effective Cafeteria Program

UNDERLYING PRINCIPLES:

- Students require a "break" in their day to socialize, let off steam, and make appropriate choices within a "menu" of possibilities.

- Privileges are earned.

- The effective cafeteria *program* facilitates instruction.

- The effective cafeteria program in and of itself is a learning opportunity.

REQUIREMENTS:

- Clearly established and consistently implemented guidelines.

- Cafeteria personnel who recognize the value of this program and who choose to make a positive difference.

- Individual and group accountability.

- A clear structure...with clear choices.

- A "menu" of activities.

HOW IT WORKS:

- Establish and inform students of regulations and why they are in place.

- Identify the privileges students will *earn* as a result of following the regulations.

- These privileges could include:
  outside volleyball/sports activities
  going to a supervised open gym/fitness center
  playing table tennis
  a room for board games
  visiting the library, computer room

- Periodically reinforce the reasons for the regulations and praise the group for following them.

- Remove the privileges for a short time should the group (or individuals) lose sight of the cooperation that is expected.

Earning privileges within the parameters of a well-defined structure – a program such as this one rewards positive behavior and gives students the opportunity to let off some steam and be refreshed for the afternoon classes which follow. No magic here – just a solid application strategy. If you tailor it to your situation it will really work.

ADOLESCENCE: A PHILOSOPHIC AND VISUAL LOOK

The "King of the One Liners," comedian Henny Youngman, was purported to have said, "All generalizations including this one are false." This commentary seems to apply to adolescence. For the image of the adolescent, society's views of what the adolescent is like, represents a pastiche of impressions and no one single thing. N. E. Kirkpatrick developed this description that captures the nature of adolescents.

> The adolescent is trying to determine who he is, to decide what he wants to become, to appraise his chances for achieving his goals, and to develop the will of self confidence to implement his decisions. He is idealistic and future oriented. He is trying to learn to face his problems and to develop the self confidence and the skills for solving them. He highly values independence, and still there are times when he wants to be dependent. He usually wants to please his significant others, but he does not always convey this notion to them. He recognizes the value of specific limits (especially when he can define them), and he wants to accept responsibility for maintaining the limits, but he also feels more secure when he knows that his significant others can take over and enforce the limits when he cannot do so. As his referent group shifts from his family, and the institutions which he associates with his family, to his peers, he questions values and behaviors which he previously accepted...especially those which suggest phoniness or hypocrisy on the part of his significant adults.

"The Mental Hygiene of Adolescents in Anglo-American Culture,"
in *Mental Hygiene*, 1952.

Notwithstanding Henny Youngman's comments, Kirkpatrick's generalizations are right on target. Another generalization is that adolescence is the most critical period of life as far as society as a whole is concerned. The tremendous impact of this period on the factors that determine one's behavior makes early adolescence of fundamental importance in shaping the destiny of a new generation. In Chapter 1 we discussed students' potential impact on the quality of life of our water planet as they confidently applied knowledge to a course of action. Understanding and mediating the conflicting forces of the adolescent's period of storm and stress enables the educator to positively influence the child's process of learning

Erikson's theory of human development placed the adolescent at the stage of *identity development* and *role clarification*. Adolescence is prominently characterized by physical, social, and emotional changes that are reflected in all facets of behavior. Some studies indicate that 30% of all adolescents avoid major problems in adjustment. For most, this is the time when the child struggles for a stable sense of self.

On a more subtle and unconscious plane, the process of pubescence affects the development of social behavior, interests, and the quality of one's affective life. I smile when I think of the time when our sons were 7 and 8 1/2 years of age. Their babysitters, mature "men" of 13 and 14, would revel in the opportunity to "sit" for the Hoff boys so they too could play with their toys, or go hide-'n-seek, or dig in the dirt with Tonka trucks. In that setting it was okay for them to be little. Both they and our boys loved it. That's what was meant when the notion that we hurry our kids into maturity was previously shared. Consider this Halloween cartoon as reflective of this point.

As adolescents define who they are, movement toward the development of proper self-understanding is often conflicted. Psychoanalytic theory indicates that through the onset of puberty, resurgence of oedipal conflicts for the boy and pre-oedipal pressures for the girl exist. As the adolescent mediates the forces between the *id* and *super ego* in searching for his ego ideal, he is often confused and conflicted. He yearns to be little but plays the "expected" role of being grown up.

TASKS OF ADOLESCENCE

Knowledgeable educators need to better understand the broad brush strokes presented by Erik Erikson (1968) in defining the tasks of adolescence. As our in-between-agers move from childhood to adulthood they confront four tasks.

- acceptance of physical changes
- attainment of identity
- achievement of independence
- transition of thinking skills

1. Acceptance of Physical Changes

Picture the seventh grade boy who had been asked to recite Patrick Henry's historic speech at a bicentennial program in 1976. As the youngster nervously stood before an audience of parents he became confused and blurted out...

Give me puberty or give me death.

Adolescents' emotions often stem from their physical development.

This malapropism, recounted by James Dobson, gives us a smile...but the message is clear. The accomplishment of a number of critically important developmental tasks stem from the physiological changes which puberty engenders. A new flood of subjective impulses are brought on by the move (or lack thereof) to developing genital and emotional maturity. In childhood the body must be mastered; in latency, the environment; and in adolescence, the emotions. In responding to bodily changes, emotions run rampant for adolescent kids.

Those who work with adolescents are well aware that some of their students look like 9 year olds, while some have the physical maturity of 17 year old men and women. Whatever they look like, most don't feel good inside about what's happening to them on the outside. For example, only 5% of all adolescent females feel good about their bodies. Just 6% of all adult women have good feelings about their bodies (Cassel, 1980). Many women never lose those negative feelings that developed in adolescence; feelings that stem from emotional reactions to physical changes.

Sudden growth and tremors of forces awakening inside challenge the adolescent's perception of the imagined perfectionism of an earlier age. Things are happening (or worse yet not happening) that due to the teenager's egocentrism are hard to understand. This insecurity is all around them in their referent peer group but they cannot see the forest from the trees of their own self-preoccupation. Their lenses are clearly directed inward. Sad? Not really – it is a part of the natural process of growth and development.

Body parts grow at uneven rates during the early adolescent years as well. It seems that many of our kids go away for winter recess only to return sporting noses that make them look as if they are eating bananas! The sudden spurt in the growth of a teenage boy is not matched with concomitant growth in the size of the heart. This muscle takes longer to develop. It works harder to send oxygen and nutrients to a wider mass of cells. Some argue that this process causes "gray outs" when the "Huh?" phase occurs regularly. And while the heart is playing "catch up," the teenager moves more slowly, has lapses in energy and demonstrates fitful periods of restlessness and seeming apathy.

This latter element is exacerbated by the youngster's inability, unwillingness, and/or insecurity to openly communicate. The early adolescent is particularly prone to become more thin-skinned, irritable, and emotionally fragile. Unpredictable explosions and mood swings occur with regularity. The in-between-ager doesn't understand what's going on. And the adults in his life, who have long distanced themselves from recollections of their own adolescence, do not understand what's going on either.

Physiology affects students' functioning in the school setting also. For example, their hips are not fully formed yet and the sciatic nerve is close to the surface. It is uncomfortable for them to sit for long periods of time. And how does the traditional school provide for this reality? By wedging kids into hard plastic and metal devices for up to 45 minutes at a time. These desk/chair combinations seem to be designed to make the room easier to clean and for the adults to arrange neat and orderly rows than for the kids who sit in them.

One of the popular exercises in a week-long institute for educators is the **Design a Chair/Learning Station** project. The participants (not encumbered by financial restraints) are given carte blanche to design a location that responds to adolescents' physiological development and the teacher's enlightened instructional perspective. Ernie Pollman created this learning station.

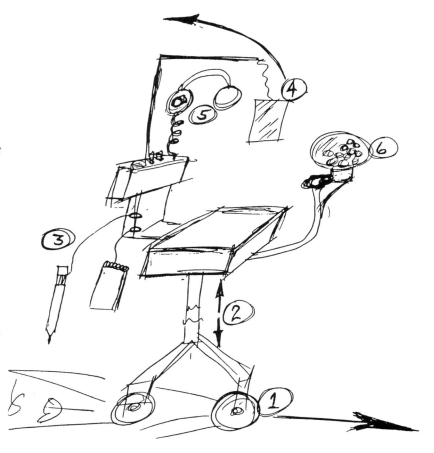

1. Wheels for mobility of social interaction.

2. Adjustable height for growth spurts.

3. Materials anchored so they don't become lost.

4. Mirror will automatically retract when the bell rings to start class.

5. Headphones & tape of directions so you don't have to repeat them.

6. Gumball machine dispenses a gumball for every correct answer.

A whimsical, interesting creation. Yet, many of Ernie's ideas make sense. We need to do more of this type of thinking to release the mental locks which inhibit our creativity. As Horace Walpole said:

> *Imagination was given to man to compensate him for what he is not.*
> *A sense of humor was provided to console him for what he is.*

No matter what turmoil teenagers undergo during this time of massive physical upheaval, our job as teachers, as their **significant others**, is to validate them with **unconditional positive regard**. They need to know that despite their sense of physical awkwardness we do indeed value them. Valuing the individual, adapting our instruction and classrooms (e.g.: recognizing that movement and variety are essential ingredients of an effective classroom) are crucial to the in-between-agers' school success. The nurturance of the teacher in an enabling classroom environment helps ease the adolescent's confrontation with this important phase of development and "greases" the wheels for the task of IDENTITY ATTAINMENT.

2. Attainment of Identity

Erikson's second major developmental task of adolescence is the attainment of identity. Whether identified as the devil's representatives in the educational system or as those who view themselves as unloved, rejected and/or misunderstood, adolescents are who they are in a period of tremendous internal turmoil and self questioning. There is extraordinary elasticity of psychological movement underlying the diversity of the adolescent period.

*There's a season
for beginnings
When the world
is fresh and new,
When we shape our dreams
of all the things
We plan and hope to do...*

*There's a season
for maturing
When we think
and work and grow,
And a season
for harvesting
Of all we've come to know...
And each successive season
Grows still richer
Than the last
As treasures
of the present
Add to memories
of the past.*

– Karen Raun

Adolescents often show their independence by the clothing they wear and the hairstyles they choose.

Confused...they seek "anchors" for the development of their personality. And belonging to the family of mankind, the adolescent naturally seeks validation from other humans. All of us have a basic need to identify ourselves as a separate, unique, distinctive human being – yet this behavior is influenced and validated by others.

Theoreticians indicate that the adolescent is in a period of working toward a personal identity and ego-consciousness. This identity or status can only be achieved within the context of societal relationships. Adolescents validate their worth via comparisons to others.

I would trade certain parts of my body were I to be able to grow hair above my eyebrows. In the 1990's the coiffures of our adolescents (e.g.: razor slash marks, sculpted bizarre forms; shaving off what I would so dearly cherish) defy adult sensibilities. Adolescents view peers, rock stars, and athletes with these hairstyles and either follow suit or fantasize about doing so.

Sometimes the best way to stand out is to blend in.

We need to understand that kids, including ones who conform in most ways, use their bodies/hair styles to demonstrate their uniqueness and rebellion. (At one time it was said that if you don't have at least some kids with green hair in your school, you don't have a creative environment.) And adolescents "put one another down" if their style is different from that of their referent group. They invalidate others to make their own stock (status) more valuable. If they are the "in-crowd" their influence and approval are beacons to the others.

This testing of roles and personal experimentation among peers is a natural part of this age group's adaptation process. They desire to gain social acceptance and status with their friends. This drive is a prime motivator for the conformity behavior that teenagers so desperately seek as they pursue their own personal identity.

Messages to friends are expressed on the You're Special Board

Trial and error, experimentation, and the process of making choices help to define the adolescent's identity. Feedback about choice helps to encourage, modify and/or discourage their ability to pursue options. Painful criticism can also create a personal aversion to making choices. The example of Lucy is undeniable in this regard.

PEANUTS Reprinted by permission of UFS, Inc.

We spoke previously of the structure that is developmentally appropriate for youngsters to become accountable for the choices they make. And those drives or intrinsic motivators determine the direction in which they grow. When asked questions they don't like or when asked questions by people who control them, teens often respond " I don't know" (mumbled swiftly so it may sound like "don'-no"). They aren't refusing to engage their brain – rather, they refrain from making a decision so they can't be held accountable (criticized). Why? Because *criticism is painful*! Accountability is important in furthering the process of identity attainment.

When adolescents do decide, then it is important for them to know that there are consequences for their decisions and that *they create* their outcomes. Here's that snowy scene the next year...

PEANUTS Reprinted by permission of UFS, Inc.

Linus realized in both cartoons that the satisfaction derived from his behavior would not be worth the pain Lucy would mete out! He responded accordingly.

Strength of character comes when people recognize that they cause outcomes from decisions they make. Power comes from that formula. Powerlessness is a strong element of the passive or dysfunctional individual; one who comes to feel that powerful forces in the universe have conspired to do *this* to me! (Whatever *this* may be.) Linus received feedback from Lucy and miraculously retrieved the thrown snowball before he had to deal with the outcome that his decision would have caused.

Strength in identity attainment comes from an **internal** locus of control (*I* control my outcomes) rather than an **external** one (*They* did this to me). And remember that when identity is not clearly attained, identity confusion occurs and that confusion can predominate throughout the person's entire life.

In the decision making process the valuing of the individual through unconditional positive regard is of paramount importance. Maslow (1943) described the self-actualized person as one whose inherent potential is fulfilled. Giving unconditional positive regard to the adolescent permits the educator to gain credibility with the student; which enables the teacher to provide open and honest feedback. This circular process increases the likelihood that the individual will accept new information. The potential for learning, growth, and self-actualization is enhanced when the individual is valued. Hazel does it well.

HAZEL

"YOU I like. However...your **SHADOW!**"

The individual has been unconditionally regarded ("You I like...") – Yet the behavior is criticized ("However, your shadow"). Effective disciplinary programs have this understanding as their cornerstone. They know that in order to make gains, the student has to understand that he is accountable for his decisions – and that as a valued human being, he has worth and accountability to the group, his teachers, and himself. This is both personal identity and identity within the organization. Students who "own" their actions are capable of making a positive difference in their schools, classrooms and most importantly in their own lives.

So as adolescents figure out who they are, and what they can become, they lean on others to obtain a sense of worth, a sense of identity. Professionally we need to be in touch with our hot buttons in order to see beyond the moment and help our students lift off the launch pad as they stand on the staging ground of their adulthood.

Responsible feedback helps to enhance the adolescent's perception of self. And a strong self-concept provides a sense of continuity which is central to the process of personality maturation and identity attainment. Bronfenbrenner said that every one of us comes into the world and wants to be prized. We never lose that. It is our challenge to keep that fact in focus and to legitimately prize each child we teach.

Students know when their teachers care about them. Former New York State English Teacher of the Year, Ron Vitale, demonstrates that fact day in and day out with his students.

3. Achievement of Independence

This developmental task involves breaking away from earlier ties and designating a life task, social role, and identity. The significance of adolescence lies in the struggle to attain independence. The typical teen attempts to abandon his childhood. He seeks a new ego ideal and explores new value systems in order to formulate what he considers to be an adult ideal. He is naturally preoccupied with himself rather than with other people or activities that are related to his developing self.

This stage is often stressful because the painful reality is that the present is chaotic. Turning inward the adolescent faces the ***Narcissistic Stage***. This stage is personified by the Personal Fable whose litany goes something like this; "*I* can drink all I want; *I* won't get pregnant if I have sex for the first time; *I* can speed and nothing will happen to me."

A tragedy hit one of our high school communities a few years ago. Three high school students left their closed campus and lingered too long at the local fast food restaurant. Noticing the lateness of the hour, they drove rapidly back to school...found traffic backed up near an intersection, drove on the shoulder of the highway...hit a pole and were killed. Three days later the school closed early to permit the grief stricken student body to attend a memorial service. Following the end of a touching ceremony, the students hopped into their cars and sped away at breakneck speed, tires squealing. They acted as if they were invulnerable, driving on the shoulder of the same highway where their classmates' lives had so tragically ended. While this age is gaining the capacity to intellectually understand cause and effect relationships, their actions don't always demonstrate this achievement. Their intense egocentricism causes them to play to an "imaginary world." These kids view themselves as indestructible immortal human beings. But they aren't. This is known as the personal fable. Greater stability occurs in later teen years. Yet narcissism as personified by the personal fable is another developmental reality.

Research and much cumulative experience validates the position that if you truly reach students prior to their 15th birthday, you will make a lasting difference in their lives. It is more difficult to influence youngsters who are in this narcissistic stage; but not impossible, just *difficult*. Their inward focus *can* be accessed by a significant other, but not by one whose being is not admired or respected.

In tough financial times that awareness might cause us to rethink the formulae under which we allocate our resources. Social work intervention and counseling efforts are far more effective at the middle school level in making a difference in the lives of our children than they are at the high school level. Just as Head Start and similar preschool strategies improve academic performance in the early grades and pay dividends over time, personality and character formation intervention at the middle will do the same. The commercial for auto repair; "Pay me now...or pay me later" is applicable. A year of preschool costs an average of $3,000 per child; a year of effective/intensive counseling intervention in the middle grades costs approximately $450 per child; while a year in prison amounts to $16,500. We can and must choose.

As adolescents move toward *independence*, parents and educators dramatically impact on the development of the self-concept. By approving or disapproving, helping or blocking, these significant others provide the source material by which children learn to value and accept themselves. When they accept and value their worth, a circular reinforcement process is set in motion – for they in turn accept and value others. As adolescents mature within a nurturing environment, they acquire sensitivities and skills that lead them to believe they can cope independently.

And when children are not raised within this type of environment, when their needs go unheeded, they will turn on the world that neglected them. Parental indifference to adolescents can have devastating consequences. This is true whether the neglect is caused by the demands of their jobs, a failing relationship, or poor economic circumstances.

How frequent are parental contacts with their children? Guess the amount of time the *typical suburban father* spends in daily conversation with his teenager. I don't mean time sitting around the television set or acting like passing ships in the course of completing the morning routine. Time spent in conversation or interaction is what's called for.

If you said less than an hour, you are slightly warm. If you said less than a half hour, you are warmer. Less than 15 minutes, you're getting hot. Less than 5 minutes? Almost there. Less than two minutes. Correct. Studies suggest that the typical suburban father spends approximately 1 minute and 50 seconds a day in conversation with his teenager. And of that time, approximately 2/3's of it is spent in negative dialog – "Did you take out the garbage yet?" "Did you get the leaves raked?" And so forth. SHOCKING! DISCOURAGING.

Charles Schaefer (1979) conducted a study of 300 7th and 8th graders. Of a father's 6.1 waking hours at home, student diaries indicated an interaction time of 7 minutes per week. He cites a study by Daniel Brown (1979) indicating interactive time of 12 1/2 minutes per day with 2/3's of that time in negative, critical interaction. Though the studies vary, the seriousness of the data gives one pause for concern. Psychologists indicate that a minimum of 15 minutes a day of parental attention is necessary to enhance positive feelings of self-worth for each child.

**Today They are Ours.
Tomorrow the World is Theirs.**

These statistics are chilling. What do we do about them? What questions must we ask in searching for answers that will guide us in working with a generation of children whose boundaries have been too loosely drawn? There must be no debate on whether we *should* teach values to our students – the debate must be *how* should we help students develop values that will lead to success in life. As we commit to this task it is essential to keep in mind that children are mirrors of the priorities and principles their parents and teachers have provided them. As the adolescent moves toward Independence, it will ever be thus.

The illustration "Today They Are Ours. Tomorrow the World is Theirs" when shown to a group of 5th grade students elicited the response that it was, "A group of kids on the playground holding up a big ball." Close, but no cigar. A few days later the same transparency was shown to a class of 8th graders. They described it as. "A group of young adults, possibly at recess, holding aloft a depictation of the Earth." (Their teacher was heavily into vocabulary development.) Three short years but a tremendously broadened perspective. This recollection helps set the stage for Erikson's last task of adolescent development.

4. Transition of Thinking Skills

The difference between adolescents' ability to perceive the world around them is illustrated by this anecdote.

> *Three students, a sixth, seventh, and eighth grader were walking down Main Street at dusk. The sixth grader glanced at a house and behind a translucent shade noticed the silhouette of two people in close physical embrace. Startled, she exclaimed..."Oooo, look at those people – they're fighting!" The seventh grader replied..."No silly, they're making love!"*
>
> *The eighth grader paused and matter-of-factly said..."Yes and rather poorly."*

Middle grades children evidence tremendous growth in their ability to process information and interpret the world in which they live. For the most part by 16 years of age the brain has fully matured. The only difference from the adult thought process at this point is experience and content. Narrowing this gap will be achieved through interactions with the environment and through further schooling.

Reprinted with special permission of King Features Syndicate, Inc.

Many adolescents experience a change from concrete operational thought patterns to an increased capability to deal with abstractions. Some never will if not enticed and challenged to think. While approximately half of all people make the jump to abstract thinking by their adult years, Hagar clearly is not among them!

Conrad Toepfer tells the story of a colleague, one venerated Doctor of Classical Literature at SUNY Buffalo. The professor, a fastidious person in every sense of the word, had just completed the construction of a new cement walkway to the side entrance of his home. The job was a masterpiece – perfect in every way. The academician turned away for a moment only to have his neighbor's child drive his tricycle, towing a wagon, followed by his St. Bernard, drive the entire length of the wet surface. Crestfallen, the professor lamented...

Frankly, I prefer children in the abstract; not in the CONCRETE!

In school we also prefer students who are in the abstract. They are far easier to reach; they understand our wit and validate our wisdom. Given a choice, many teachers repudiate the great unwashed who are mired in the concrete. They cling to tracked groupings of students and eagerly anticipate the one class each day with the gifted that saves their sanity.

Organizationally we often set students up for failure – through homogeneous grouping patterns and/or by not considering the cognitive level that many of our instructional activities require. We need to acknowledge that every child has a gift and all can learn – albeit in different ways and at different times.

We presume our kids are capable of inductive/deductive reasoning. Yet fewer than 30% of 8th graders give evidence of this fact (Garvin, 1989). The effective teacher also recognizes that predetermined biases about how much (or how little) a child can learn are deadly to what a student can often achieve. The effective teacher knows that abstractions are made real via clear, concrete examples that enable the learner to experience success.

The concept of population density is taught at some point in the middle grades social studies curriculum. It may be a portion of the "around the world in 80 days" approach to global studies or some aspect of colonization or through the demographic study of waves of immigration. While students can parrot back the definition of the terms we need to ask, do they really understand the abstraction? The teacher who is not content with memorization and who knows that learning is a moving experience might consider these examples which utilize instructional techniques that are targeted to the student's differing learning styles.

• The desired body of knowledge (terms, content, etc.) is initially presented to the group by the teacher.

• A print by American artist, Georgia O'Keeffe, of a New Mexico landscape is displayed. Students are asked to describe what they see, and what they feel (vis-a-vis the open airy feeling the work generates).

• A second print by Pablo Picasso is shown. It is his cubist period (around 1906) depicting congested space and overlapped images. What do they see? What do they feel? What comparisons to the O'Keeffe print can they make? (Again vis-a-vis the concept of openness and density.)

• Two pieces of music are played. The first is Grofe's **Grand Canyon Suite** featuring a clip of **"On The Trail."** What images does this music create for you? What do you "see" as a result of this auditory image? The second piece is Gershwin's **American in Paris**. The obvious sounds of the city reach the students' ears. Car horns, blaring noises, paints a dramatically different image than the Western scene that was identified in the first musical segment. What image is conveyed? What are some of the differences that the music portrays?

• The front of the room is cleared – except for 3 chairs. The teacher puts the population (23,667,902 in 1980) and number of square miles (156,740) of California on the board. The teacher indicates that each chair represents roughly 50,000 square miles.

Two volunteers are secured. They sit on two of the chairs (representing 11,900,000 people). The teacher says that this represents the *population density* of California. What do you see. What information is depicted?

The population (119 million) and number of square miles (143,706) of Japan are put on the board. Ten volunteers are secured. All 10 are asked to sit on the three chairs – somehow. When the organized chaos and giggling subsides, the same questions are presented. What do you see?, what information is depicted? What do you understand about *population density* as a result of these examples?

A demonstration of population density makes an abstract concept meaningful.

Applicaton and discussion may be then pursued in a variety of directions. But one thing is clear. The students have heard, visualized, and *been a part of population density*. They will not easily lose the concept – and the thought process the teacher walked them through.

This teacher used clear examples, physically engaged students in the lesson, and used multiple modalities so students could process information concretely. He was aware that using auditory, visual, and kinesthetic teaching enabled students to connect and master key concepts. Studies indicate that 20% of our students learn best when teachers share information verbally (auditorily); 35% learn best when given hands on tasks (kinesthetically); and 45% learn best when pictures and media are heavily used (visually). (Garvin 1989)

A number of Western New York State kids were asked to identify the features they admired in their "best" teachers. They listed many; a sense of humor. interesting, energetic, encouraging, and possessing the ability to get the best work out of each pupil. These were a few of the more consistently mentioned qualities. In one school a group of forty 6th, 7th and 8th grade student council representatives were describing their best teachers to me. One sixth grader enthusiastically shared...

You know, I like it when they put DIAPHRAGMS on the board. A seventh grader nodded his agreement and concurred. *Yeah, I like those pictures, too.* Meanwhile, the 8th graders were on the floor, convulsed with laughter. A true story.

Kids in the middle school bring different understanding and experience levels "to the table." Visual learners like diagrams, auditory learners love the reinforcement that comes with the creative use of music as a backdrop to their learning. And like the proverbial duck, kinesthetic learners take to water when given hands-on tasks to perform.

Young adolescents learn best when their hands and mouths can be involved – appropriately.

Reprinted with special permission of King Features Syndicate, Inc.

Like Hagar, the 6th and 7th graders in the previous story obviously didn't have the same vocabulary as the 8th graders. And though the topics may be different, it is incumbent on us to provide students with the learning experiences that can have them increase their capacity to understand, interpret, and influence the world around them.

Reprinted with special permission of King Features Syndicate, Inc.

In order to create WIN-ners, our kids cannot "have no idea!" They need to be able to confidently apply their learning to a realistic course of action. In so doing, we can make a dramatic impact on learners and how they influence the quality of their lives.

CROCK   By Rechin & Wilder

Reprinted with special permission of King Features Syndicate, Inc.

The school has the capacity to introduce youngsters to knowledge that can form the base of their evolving socio-psychological and philosophical conceptualization of the world. Attempting to positively influence the lives of students at this critical time of development is a great challenge. Adolescents face major tasks:

1. Understanding and accepting physical changes
2. Moving confidently in the definition and attainment of their identity
3. Fulfilling their destiny by achieving independence
4. Broadening their capacity to better understand and influence the world in which they live.

The empowered school influences students positively and helps them achieve these developmental tasks. In a time when the number of alienated youth is mushrooming in a time when improper choices could mean irreversible consequences and the loss of many lives in a time when dysfunctional families are a stark reality in a time where models for our youth come from the tube rather than the dinner table, we who choose to work with children in their formative times of development, must make a significant difference through the "World of School."

To do so requires that we are convinced of our abilities to make a difference, possess the personal and professional skills to make a difference, have a clear understanding of ourselves – our needs, biases, and are willing to make a thorough analysis of how we can magnify our talents to make that difference.

The next chapter provides practical suggestions for taking stock of who we are; for rolling aside the stones that impede our journey, and for enabling us to become what we must be in order to make a significant difference in the lives of our students, our colleagues, and ourselves. 🍎

Chapter 3

Understanding you: Less than perfect...but very special

> *The story is told that during the Dark Ages, the repository of all knowledge was the monastery and that the answer to all questions could be found in the books of centuries past. Now it so happened that one day a visitor to the monastery thought, "I wonder, how many teeth are in a horse's mouth?" The keepers of all knowledge (the monks) responded in the time-tested manner to which they addressed all questions – they checked the books. They checked the books of the East that had been brought by Marco Polo. They checked the books of the New World (Africa). They checked the books of Europe. In no source was the number of teeth that were in a horse's mouth revealed. So they did what the prevailing logic of the time called for, they deduced... THERE WERE NO TEETH IN A HORSE'S MOUTH!*

Individuals differ greatly in their approach to new ideas and change. This fact is true in all organizations and certainly in the place we call school.

Understandably, many school people like the monks in the above fable, fall into patterns that preclude the consideration of new ways of thinking – alternatives which challenge past assumptions, habits, or procedures. Actually counting the number of teeth in a horse's mouth would have been a logical step for the clerics, but it would have altered the pattern they had followed for centuries. And **habit** more than any other factor retards the forward movement of an organization. "But we've always done it that way" is the common response.

Today, perhaps more than ever before, we need to test the assumptions and patterns that have governed our thinking. We need to address analytically the need to reform our schools. The place to begin is within each of us.

How you confront change, how you obtain clearer insights about yourself, and how you can challenge assumptions that inhibit the development of an empowered school are discussed in this chapter.

The main character in Washington Irving's classic story, *The Legend of Sleepy Hollow*, Rip Van Winkle was said to have slept for nearly twenty years. An educational sidebar to that old tale goes something like this:

> *After Rip had awakened following years of blissful slumber, he ambled along the road returning to the village of his youth. Startled by a loud noise – one unlike any he had heard before – he hid behind a bush just as a huge mechanical monster*

came roaring over a hill spewing fumes, riding on what appeared to be 16 wheels and blaring a horn as it passed. Sweating profusely from the sight of this strange apparition, Rip continued his journey. Startled again by another sound, he retreated to the protection of a bush, only to see a huge metallic bird soaring in the sky. Rip thought to himself, I must have slept longer than I thought for these frightening things had not existed before. Continuing on, Rip spied a building in the distance. Nearing it he smiled a bit for he knew it was a school. When he stepped inside a classroom, he breathed a sigh of relief for this classroom hadn't changed at all!

A tongue in cheek interpretation of a classic tale, but one with a clear moral. The school hasn't changed as have other aspects of our lives.

When Rip entered the school he viewed the type of classroom that rooms have been patterned after since the late 1800's. And one wonders whether we have addressed the pattern of our organizations with an eye toward continued development. For if things have changed little do we perpetuate *what is* while sacrificing *what could be*?

Though the story is obviously fictitious, it contains kernels of truth. Realistically, many patterns, habits and procedures are self-perpetuating and difficult to alter. Of course, many of them appear to work quite well, so one might ask, why change them?

Reprinted with permission of Ford Button

"Our architect has come up with an interesting concept in building design that might create an atmosphere in which students could achieve excellence."

Alfred North Whitehead said, "There are two choices open to mankind — **advance** or **decadence**." Don Essig made the same point differently. "The only difference between being in a rut and being in your grave is the depth of the hole!"

It is known generally that American schools operate approximately twenty-five to fifty years behind the profession's knowledge base. Since we lag in applying our knowledge to educational actions, it is desirable that we know why this may be true, but very important that we provide suggestions designed to alter this reality. We need, then, to address why we haven't advanced our thinking to institute new practices and to eliminate unsuccessful ones; to get out of the *ruts* that have restricted our thinking.

PERFECTIONISM

The modern classroom was first developed in Quincy, Massachusetts long, long ago. The "Quincy Box" staked out territory within which a teacher could autonomously direct the flow of instruction. Four walls, with a door leading to a central corridor, enabled the teacher to provide a safe, orderly environment, wherein *control* would be achieved with minimal disruption. It worked. It also created a sense of isolation in which individual teachers could do their "own thing" without the awareness or assistance of colleagues. The early classroom soon became the norm and the standard of order and control became deeply woven into the fabric of American education. (This is not to say that control and order are unnecessary elements in the scheme of things. Obviously they are.)

Unfortunately control issues often create isolation, minimal collegial inter-action, and individual rather than collaborative behavior on the part of teachers. The old Quincy model is still alive and well in American schooling as are the patterns it helped to create.

As professional educators we need to understand the relationship of control issues to organizational empowerment. In order to establish a more effective arena for growth and analysis we need to face who we are (present), and what factors influenced us (past), before we can effectively consider what we can become (future.)

PERFECTIONISM is one of the most damaging inhibitors of individual and organizational growth. Whether one personally falls into this category or not, it is important to understand the concept. Understanding assists colleagues, ourselves, and our schools to achieve an awareness level that encourages forward movement – movement away from regulated patterns that breaks habit and leads both individuals and organizations to enhanced growth opportunities.

The *New Webster Encyclopedic Dictionary of the English Language* defines PERFECT as...

> Brought to a consummation or completion; having received and possessing all its parts; finished; completed; of the best, highest, or completest type; without blemish or defect; faultless; completely skilled.

Our interpretation of the perfectionist's world leans heavily on the insights of Jennifer James (1985) who has explored this topic with tremendous clarity.

The perfectionist feels that...if I can be absolutely perfect then others (everyone) will love me. The stark reality is that most people don't want to be around someone who is perfect. The energies of the perfectionist are spent trying to achieve perfect control and perfect order. In fact they seem to prefer order over human relationships.

In schools, which are primarily human enterprises, the perfectionist deals well with *things*. The report is in on time – the lunch money has to be collected – the attendance register must be just so. This behavior is likely to be rewarded and appreciated where these tasks are done well. This enables the perfectionist to achieve outward success...but at what expense? For it is only in later life that perfectionists realize what it has cost them, especially if the most important thing was to compete totally, to claw over others, to be on top, to be #1.

Hindsight being twenty-twenty, the perfectionist does not realize that there often is a linkage between perfectionism → criticism → and personal feelings of low self-worth. Because as flawed humans it is not possible to be perfect, without blemish, "just so" every moment of every day. Yet perfectionists are driven to achieve this mythical standard. Only in retrospection does someone who has been a perfectionist learn that one's life has been impaired because of this quest for an unattainable outcome.

Accordingly, perfectionists resist dealing with variables not readily mastered. **Change** is not only difficult but extremely threatening, so perfectionists are thrown off center and they resist. They tend to trade in criticism in order to *control* and minimize the successes of others. They are likely to undermine new initiatives in order to limit the variables with which they have to contend. Dealing with those practices and approaches they have mastered, especially those that have given them prominence or "status" with others, are the variables they employ to seek their goal – to be skillful, unblemished, complete, *perfect* in the eyes of others and themselves. If the attainment of such a solitary goal becomes the pattern of interaction, an interesting cause and effect relationship is developed for the perfectionist...

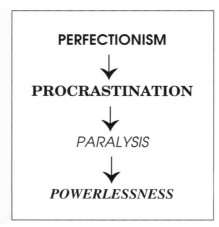

PERFECTIONISM

↓

PROCRASTINATION

↓

PARALYSIS

↓

POWERLESSNESS

When schools, which are basically arenas for human interaction, set out on a new course or seek to alter previous patterns of functioning, the perfectionist faces the linkage noted in the cartoon.

The perfectionist's inability or unwillingness to challenge new variables leads to delaying behaviors (procrastination) which in turn leads to inaction (paralysis) which leads to the key element in low self-esteem (powerlessness). When the individual thus becomes dysfunctional, the degree to which the organization can become empowered is affected. Using a parallel example, consider the impact but one dysfunctional letter of a typewriter could have on a typed passage.

XMPOWXRMXNT

"Xvxn though my typxwritxr is an old modxl, it works quitx wxll. Xxcxpt for onx kxy, that is. Thxrx arx 46 kxys that function wxll xnough, but just onx kxy not working makxs thx diffxrxncx.

"Somxtimxs likx my typxwritxr, not all thx kxys in an organization arx working propxrly. You may say, 'Wxll, I am only onx pxrson. It won't makx much diffxrxncx.' But you should bx ablx to sxx that thx group to bx xffxctivx nxxds thx activx participation of xvxry pxrson.

"So thx nxxt timx you think you arx only onx pxrson, rxmxmbxr my typxwritxr and say to yoursxlf, I am a kxy pxrson, and I am nxxdxd vxry much!"

Author unknown

Each person is important. Each person can and should make a positive difference. That is why it is important to understand the dynamics of *perfectionistic dysfunction* – for like the errant letter "e" on the typewriter, perfectionism impacts on the harmony of the organization. Just as each person can make a positive difference, so the dysfunctional individual can create an aura or tension that impacts the health of an organization.

These suggestions may prove helpful in dealing with perfectionism.

How To Deal With Perfectionism

I. Perfectionists need to understand the roots of their perfectionism.

Many perfectionists are that way because of the manner in which they were raised. Quite likely, perfectionistic adults were raised through the conditional love of their parents (e.g.: you are loved only to the degree that you meet the conditions I set.)

Let's suppose the eleven year old boy takes over the family job of mowing the lawn. He excitedly races into the house having just completed the task and says to father..." Dad, I just mowed the whole lawn!" Father, arising from the couch, asks a series of questions in rapid fire succession (not waiting for an answer).

"Did you wipe the mower and the blade clean? Did you bag the clippings and put them to the right of the driveway? Did you return the mower to the X marks in the garage? Did you...? Did you...?" The youngster, head down, returns to the garage to complete the lesser tasks that father thought to be so important. The father's questioning invalidated the child's initiative and industriousness. He made it clear that unless the task was completed to his particular standard (conditions) it was not acceptable and worthy of praise.

While conditions may be important in the sequencing of tasks to be performed, the on-going validation of a youngster's worth is essential. As models, we must be sensitive to control issues and the positive validation of our children especially when they enter into new tasks. At home we must give them unconditional love, and at school **unconditional positive regard**. We need to say to each child..."You have worth in and of yourself and your worth is not determined by what you produce."

A POEM FOR PARENTS
(and Teachers)

I've got two A's," the small boy cried,
His voice was filled with glee.
His father very bluntly asked,
"Why didn't you get three?"

"Mom, I've got the dishes done,"
The girl called from the door.
Her mother very calmly said,
"And did you sweep the floor?"

"I've mowed the grass," the tall boy said,
"And put the mower away."
His father asked him with a shrug,
"Did you clean off all the clay?"

The children in the house next door
Seemed happy and content.
The same things happened over there,
But this is how it went.

"I got two A's" the small boy cried,
His voice filled with glee.
His father proudly said, "That's great!
I'm glad you live with me!"

"Mom, I've got the dishes done,"
The girl called from the door.
Her mother smiled and softly said,
"Each day I love you more."

"I've mowed the grass," the tall boy said,
"And put the mower away."
His father answered with much joy,
"You've made my happy day."

Children deserve a little praise,
For tasks they're asked to do.
If they're to lead a happy life,
So much depends on you.

Author unknown

Adults also need a little praise as well. Each of us enters the world wanting to be prized – and we never lose that.

II. Perfectionists need to understand the difference between high standards and perfectionism.

There is an enormous difference between high standards which you can work toward and feel real satisfaction in achieving and perfection which is an absolute illusion. The saying goes: We chase perfection so we can catch excellence.

The difference is that the productive, well adjusted person competes within him/herself for new gains rather than competing with a mythical standard of perfection. To the non-perfectionist the **process** of growth is critical; to the perfectionist the **outcome** is the criterion that counts.

Robert Ferchat from Northern Telecom Canada Ltd. provided an interesting perspective on high standards. He noted that...

If people got things right 99% of the time

- At least 200,000 wrong prescriptions would be filled each year...
- There would be 9 misspelled words on every page in a magazine...
- We'd have unsafe drinking water 4 times a year...
- There would be no telephone service for 15 minutes each day...

Obviously we don't desire our pharmacist to be right only 99% of the time. And unless we have a teenage daughter at home, we probably wouldn't want the inconvenience of interrupted telephone service. Yet as educators, would we be uncomfortable if 99% of our children consistently performed above statistical expectations on a norm referenced test?

If our students consistently performed above expectations, we would raise our expectations. We would renorm the tests because we would have broken the inviolacy of the "Bell Shaped Curve." Perfectionistic thinking, although well-intended, drives our schools and the "unattainable" often directs the evaluation of our efforts.

As educators we face multiple inconsistencies in addressing high standards. While we drive ourselves to have each of our students achieve success, we must wonder if it is ethically correct for us to

Reprinted with special permission of King Features Syndicate, Inc.

expect less than 100%? This anomaly drives the perfectionist to high frustration levels. How do we reach perfection yet deal with people and circumstances which are far less than perfect. Understanding ourselves and our interactions with others is crucial to the empowerment of all organizations.

Our focus must be thus – to aspire to 100% success yet to both value and refine the process even though we may fall short of our target. We must value our students and ourselves and recognize that perfection is an illusion which must not get in the way of those goals that are achievable.

III. Perfectionists need to be less critical and judgmental of others and themselves.

> ### *To Wonder Woman and Captain Marvel*
>
> *Everybody knows*
> *You can't be all things to all people.*
> *You can't do all things at once.*
> *You can't do all things equally well.*
> *Your humanity is showing, just like everyone else's.*
>
> *So...*
>
> *You have to find out who you are, and be that.*
> *You have to decide what comes first and do that.*
> *You have to discover your strengths, and then use them.*
> *You have to learn to compete with others, because*
> *No one else is in the contest of "being you."*
>
> *Then...*
>
> *You will have learned to accept your own uniqueness.*
> *You will have learned to set priorities and make decisions.*
> *You will have learned to live with your limitations.*
> *You will have learned to give yourself the respect that is due.*
> *And you'll be a most vital mortal.*
>
> *Dare to believe...*
>
> *That you are a wonderful, unique person.*
> *That you are a once-in-all-history event.*
> *That it's more than a right – it's your duty – to be who you are.*
> *That life is not a problem to solve, but a gift to cherish.*
> *And you'll be able to stay one up on what used to get you down.*
>
> *– Robert W. Lind*

Getting in touch with yourself, your motives, your habits, your needs is important. Accordingly, perfectionists must analyze and understand that the manner in which they were brought up may be driving their adult behaviors and current attitudes. The critical nature of the perfectionist is targeted to lowering the stock of others. Relaxing one's judgmental tendencies may be initially difficult, but like the journey of a thousand miles, it begins with the first step. It is important to assess habits and circles of friends who tend to reinforce those critical behaviors that perfectionists often display. Each of us has a role in gently bringing this understanding to the consciousness of our perfectionistic brethren.

IV. Perfectionists need to be able to retreat to a safe harbor.

In the blemished world of real schools, there are many inconsistencies, many variables over which one has no control. The budget is developed by others, the kids aren't properly prepared, there are too many tests, paper work abounds, assemblies interrupt instruction, etc., etc. Consequently perfectionists try to limit the variables of their world in order to create the needed order in life.

We all need some routines and orderliness. To have little or no control over our activities and environment creates dysfunction within an individual. It is a case of degree. We all want to be the captain of our ship with favorable winds to steer our course. Yet despite this desire, winds vary in force and direction and we all get blown off course. When that happens we look to the familiar, safe harbors to ride out the errant currents or winds that disorient us.

This fact is highly significant to perfectionists. What they need in times of storm tossed waters is a personal harbor, a refuge of calm. While some may revel in the challenge of high-seas' sailing, perfectionists do not. Knowing this, perfectionists who can function well in times of organizational change, are often in touch with their need to retreat to a safe location, a place where they can control the variables. It is not an isolated harbor that is needed, for isolation in an empowered organization is not desirable. But in order to contribute to new organizational initiatives, perfectionists need to feel secure. Security and interconnectedness are essential to organizational movement. An example of how this notion exists in the work environment, involves a teacher we'll call Jerry.

A fine teacher, Jerry was entering his early 40's with less hair and a few too many pounds. He needed to have a sense of order in his life. He genuinely loved his students and his subject but was unable to assess his own personal needs as they influenced his professional patterns. Like many of us, Jerry had fallen into habits that unconsciously drove him toward his personal ideal of perfection.

Jerry's classroom was just so, displays were hung neatly. The blinds were adjusted evenly, the cleaned chalk trays had pieces of chalk all of the same length, and the rows of desks were an engineer's dream of straight line harmony. Now even though Jerry was well liked by his students, middle grades' youngsters are prone to look for soft spots or chinks in their significant others' armor. In likening them with some justification to the fresh water fish, **Piranha**, eighth grade students have been accused of attacking others. In Jerry's case, his students discovered the teacher's Achilles' heel – his fetish for straight rows – and attacked.

Picture this. Teacher greets students and turns to write something on the board. Five students noiselessly pick desks up and move them four inches off center line in each of the rows. Teacher turns around, becomes upset, not fully knowing why. When the teacher turns to write on the board again, another group pick up desks and move them off line while original five go back into place. The teacher turns around – something's not right here. He becomes even more distraught. By now the piranha know they've got him. A few more times and poor Jerry is beaten down by the systematic attack of these 8th grade beasties striking the soft spot of his personality structure – his **perfectionism**.

After a few days of this sort of scenario Jerry asked a colleague to come have a "look-see." Something was wrong and he didn't quite know what it was. His colleague quickly discovered the cause of the problem. In a follow-up conference, Jerry looked into the mirror held by his visitor and saw what had been occurring.

Recognizing that he needed to confront the patterns that grew from his perfectionism, Jerry decided to realign the classroom desk arrangement. Actually he had wanted to pursue a change but hadn't done so because his personal habits were directing his professional decisions. The teacher assessed his personal needs, matched them with his professional role, and adjusted/adapted.

But this wasn't enough. Jerry had to personally accommodate the prevailing westerly winds of a new seating configuration but needed a sense of order while he accepted a different pattern in his professional life. Jerry's port in the storm became a lockable desk drawer. In it this fine teacher could *control the variables* that lay within. He got one of those desk organizers, the kind with many different compartments. The paper clips could now be arranged in an orderly fashion. The pencils could be sharpened and aligned with the Mogul #2 label facing up. The rubber bands could be placed in concentric circles. Here was pure perfection and whenever Jerry needed to, he could unlock the drawer and there it was just as he had left it, waiting for him like he knew it would be.

A lot of water now has passed under that bridge and more will follow. But, this teacher came to grips with the *personal* motivators that drove him and was able to make professional decisions that directly bear on improving instruction. Would these changes have occurred had the teacher not looked into the mirror of perfectionism held by a colleague? Perhaps, but the likelihood of Jerry productively addressing his tendencies would not have been as great.

Perfectionists need to have at least one harbor that can be perfect – a room in the house, a desk drawer, the plan book, whatever. Having a safe harbor enables the perfectionist to weather the perils of a new journey. We all need to recognize this condition so that we can understand and assist our colleagues and ourselves.

V. Perfectionists need to understand that misteaks (mistakes) are an acceptable reality of life.

Colleague, Dennis Boike, has a personal touchstone which helps him help others in their personal development. He suggests that if one is experiencing failure at something, declare halftime and come out for the second half ready to apply what you've learned during the first half. Many people let down after they've faced defeat, but by declaring a second half one can change the word "failure" to "feedback." And feedback is the stuff that enables the effective player to redirect energy to obtain success.

The litany of successful people is rooted in "feedback."
Consider the following:

Occurance	Age
Failed in business	22
Ran for Legislature-defeated	23
Again failed in business	24
Elected to Legislature	25
Sweetheart died	26
Had a nervous breakdown	27
Defeated for Speaker	29
Defeated for Elector	31
Defeated for Congress	34
Elected to Congress	37
Defeated for Congress	39
Defeated for Senate	46
Defeated for Vice President	47
Defeated for Senate	49
Elected President of the United States	51

That's the record of **Abraham Lincoln**!

If Lincoln expected to get it right the first time, and gave up when he failed to do so, his accomplishments would never have taken place. Lincoln must have declared numerous halftimes.

Many perfectionists having been raised on conditional love don't come out for the second half ready to enjoin the battle. They fear failure because they cannot be "loved" if they are less than perfect. Trying an approach that may be unsuccessful will often cause them to retreat from the arena. They withhold their participation to protect an aura of invincibility.

If I don't contribute, I can't be responsible for something that doesn't work.

If you participate, you may make me look bad...so I will undermine your efforts – and criticize the heck out of what you are doing!

Though these comments aren't necessarily verbalized or even consciously considered, they represent actions which become blocking patterns that are inherent in dysfunctional organizations.

Perfectionists need to know that life is a series of trial/error/feedback experiences which enables *growth* to occur. There is no way that people or organizations can improve unless they risk and reach out to connect with new patterns and new ways of looking at things. Those who refuse to alter patterns and risk, make errors of **o**mission rather than **co**mission. The old adage of the two ways to climb an oak tree applies.

One...is to climb aggressively – hand over hand.
The other...is to sit on an acorn!

If you were to visualize these examples it is obvious one works while the other is inexorably slow (and possibly quite painful.)

If inaction and failure to risk makes one safe, consider these prominent failures...

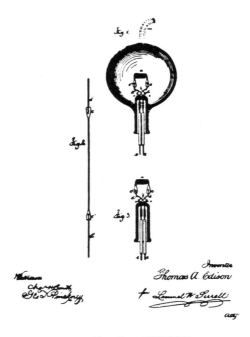

T. A. EDISON
Electric Lamp
No. 223,898.
Patented Jan. 27, 1880.

• **Albert Einstein** – who was judged to be learning disabled; incapable of effective learning.

• **Christopher Columbus** – who believed he had discovered the East Indies.

• **Rodgers and Hammerstein** – whose first work bombed so badly that they didn't collaborate for a number of years.

• **Thomas Edison** – who first discovered 1,800 ways NOT to build a lightbulb.

These individuals all took risks and challenged their own and others' assumptions, yet regained perspective when their early attempts were not successful.

Resting on one's laurels is another way perfectionists tend to interpret the world around them. While it is natural to cling to peak moments where one has dramatically succeeded, these accomplishments should be seen as **benchmarks** rather than **end points**. The saying goes, minds are like parachutes – they only function when open.

The relationship between success and openness is illustrated by the story of John Sargent, famous American artist. One of his early paintings had been highly praised by art critics. Although this work was sought after, the artist refused to sell it. Whenever he faced moments of doubt – crossroads in his personal or professional life – he contemplated that painting, and said to himself, "I painted that," and went on. Sargent subsequently had more than a few moments in the sunshine – yet he leaned on previous accomplishments to set the stage for what was to come. While *reputation* may be what you've achieved, *character* is what you do about it. Sargent had plenty of both. He used this benchmark to create future masterpieces.

Edison, using direct current (DC), founded the electrical supply industry. His success may have blinded him to the development of alternating current (AC) and that the future lay with that type of current. Was Edison a failure? Obviously not. Could he have pressed his discovery even further? Monday morning quarterbacks might say so. The "trap" is when clinging on to memories you may let the future slip by. In our empowered schools we need to take successes then build on them.

Thus, the twenty year career teacher can look around and say, "Should I repeat the same year a twenty-first time, or should I take my successes of the past, try a few new wrinkles and make my twenty-first year the best one ever?" One teacher after 33 years of successful service announced in the fall that, "This will be the final year of my teaching career – and it's going to be my best!" And it was.

L. L. Bean, Inc. of Freeport, Maine presents another success story. Their 24 hours a day customer service is legendary. In 1912 the company's founder, Leon Leonwood Bean, sold his first 100 pairs of Maine hunting shoes. They were sold with Bean's name on them and with it went his unqualified promise of customer satisfaction. But ninety pair came back with stitching that failed to hold up to the Maine woods. Despite the risk of bankruptcy Bean borrowed the money to make his refunds.

> ### 100% Guarantee
> All of our products are guaranteed to give 100% satisfaction in every way. Return anything purchased from us at any time if it proves otherwise. We will replace it, refund your purchase price or credit your credit card, as you wish. **We do not want you to have anything from L.L. Bean that is not completely satisfactory.**

Today over three-quarters of a century later, customer service is the hallmark of this company. The cornerstone of L. L. Bean's success has been the company's ability to move beyond circumstance, to lean on its fundamental integrity and continuously improve. Unlike the perfectionist who sat on an acorn, one can climb with confidence and catch brilliant rays of sunlight on the journey.

What the perfectionist needs to know is that even if he makes a mistake, others will value him. The roles of the principal and superintendent are essential in creating such an atmosphere. If an individual models a keen sensitivity to process, growth, and risk then others will emulate this open approach to

change. Perfectionists can learn when others model how to deal with new variables, even though they rarely acknowledge it.

One successful technique to help perfectionists grow was provided by a family counselor. He requires his male clients to wear two different color socks to the session. Picture it – a three piece boardroom suit, fastidiously appointed accessories, and one brown and one black sock. Though uncomfortable, the clients learn they can get through this ordeal even though they race to the parking lot to change their socks following the session.

This technique has perfectionistic people purposely making simple mistakes to learn that they can survive. Learning this helps them to confront new paradigms of thinking. Confronting new ways of interpreting the world helps both perfectionistic individuals and their organizations to grow.

VI. We all need to recognize that perfectionism is an illusion and gets in the way of achievable goals.

W. Beran Wolfe (1933) developed an approach to happiness and life. It deals with action, commitment to growth, and living life to the fullest.

> *If you observe a really happy man you will find him building a boat, writing a symphony, educating his son, growing double dahlias in his garden, or looking for dinosaur eggs in the Gobi desert. He will not be searching for happiness as if it were a collar button that has rolled under the radiator. He will have become aware that he is happy in the course of living twenty-four crowded hours of each day.*

In the empowered school – one in which the whole is greater than the sum of its parts – it is not unusual to find those who crowd a variety of talents into their personal and professional twenty-four hours. The process of validating the uniqueness and contribution of colleagues is crucial in an empowered organization. When people are respected for the things they do well, they expand their repertoire and share with others. When people share in the growth process then the isolationism engendered by habit, behavior patterns and perfectionistic thinking will be overcome. When that happens perfectionism will not become one of the molehills we trip over as we climb with confidence the mountains of our lives. And reaching peaks is what life and organizational empowerment can be all about. The climb is enhanced when we realize that **the illusion and reality of perfectionism are diametrically opposed** and pursuit of the illusion damages our efforts to achieve our goals.

BEETLE BAILEY MORT WALKER

Reprinted with special permission of King Features Syndicate, Inc.

Dare to be less than perfect, climb the oak tree and the mountains of your life with vigor, grow through the feedback that halftime permits, cling to benchmarks of success as reference points for new successes – and venture from safe harbors. In so doing you will reach an uncommon success. We all need to **explore...experiment...expand**. Our schools, colleagues and students deserve nothing less. 🍎

Chapter 4

Confronting CHANGE:
A Personal and Professional Challenge

Some have said the only ones open to change are wet babies, yet change is inevitable. Adults and students alike, then, need to have a safe, supportive environment, one in which they are willing to take risks. Clear support and encouragement is needed for one to press one's limits, to take chances, and to succeed, or to fail, without losing a sense of self-worth.

By our nature we are creatures of habit. Habits give us the sense of order that enables us to deal with the changes of life. At the same time, however, habits provide mental locks that may limit our ability to broaden our focus and grow.

In the previous chapter it was noted that through trial and error, we learn. And the attitudes that people have largely determine how they confront variables of newness and whether or not they have a willingness to grow in order to leave the ruts of their conditioning.

Phillip Schlecty (1990) has identified the pattern that has predominated in our secondary schools for many years.

> Imagine for a moment that you are an alien – a being from another galaxy – and you observe a typical American secondary school. Groups of students are moving from cell to cell at the sound of a bell. Adults are in isolated classrooms – teachers are talking 85% of the time. As an alien your conception of the American secondary school might be that of a place where relatively young people come to watch relatively old people at work!

The paradox of Schlecty's description is that although we recognize engaged activity increases student learning, we all too often accept students as passive observers within the classroom setting. This needs to change.

This chapter provides a working understanding of the concept of change, the barriers to confront, the personal focus and approaches utilized to bring change about, and the challenges faced by educators. As we remove roadblocks and head toward the empowered school we must detach ourselves and view objectively *what is* so that we might better create what *ought to be*.

> *Never doubt that a small group of thoughtful, committed citizens can change the world; indeed it's the only thing that ever has.*

> – *Margaret Mead*

Anthropologist Margaret Mead says it well in the following parable. It provides an answer when considering a course of action or where to begin.

> The Creator was once asked by an archangel where the angel should hide the "Secrets of the Universe." On the highest mountain top? "NO," was the reply. On the bottom of the deepest ocean? "NO," boomed the voice. In the center of the earth? "NO" again was the response. "Well then," asked the angel, "where shall I hide them so no one will ever discover these mysteries?"
>
> "Hide them in such a place, where no human will ever look. Hide them in such a remote place that no one will stumble upon them. Hide them in such a place that truly will escape all who quest for the great secrets."
>
> So the angel did...he hid them inside each of us!

And that is where we shall begin our search to understand one of the secrets of the universe – how to **change**. We'll look within ourselves.

When starting a workshop a technique that helps individuals come to grips with change follows. It involves active participation and provides a clear demonstration.

> "Please interlock your fingers and fold your hands together...Notice how you have folded your thumbs. Now, switch your thumbs.
>
> "Which one felt more comfortable to you? Over 90% of all people indicate that the first one did.
>
> "OK...now fold your arms across your chest... Now fold them the other way."

What invariably happens is the group breaks into laughter because a large number of the participants have trouble folding their arms the other way. The lesson is obvious. We "program" ourselves and seek comfortable patterns when completing routine tasks. Personal awareness is important to growth.

Now consider how you might react when facing a new situation that requires conscious thought. Picture this one.

Think back to the last time you were in a professional meeting with 15 or more adults. Think of the setting, the room, where you sat. Let's suppose, as in many meetings, the topic under discussion does not totally absorb you and you lose concentration for a moment. WHAM! All of a sudden something bizarre happens. The room lights go out, but instead of darkness, a golden yellow aura begins to pulse on-off, on-off, on-off, until the light remains as a constant. Steam fills the room, clogging every inch of space and every pore of your consciousness.

Though you and your colleagues wish to flee, you can't. You sit transfixed for minutes that seem like hours, in anticipation of something to give meaning to this irrational moment. "And then it happens. Defying all known laws of science, a spaceship appears. A gangplank parts the mist and lands three feet from where you sit. A boney finger cleaves the air and beckons...'Follow me, follow me.'

Would you? Would you follow the invitation of the boney finger and walk up the gangplank? If you are like 95% of the people asked this question of, you wouldn't. Approximately 5% say 'Sure – why not; I've had a rough week, my social calendar isn't too full and I'll do just about anything to get out of this meeting!' Such folks are decidedly in the minority.

Carrying this analysis further, about 40% answer in the affirmative when asked: "Now if those few who went up the gangplank and came back from the ship then said...'This is fantastic, you've got to come on up here to see this!'...*How many of you would now follow?*"

Have you answered affirmatively yet? If not, you are in the clear majority! You are one who would not go...no way, never! Now let's suppose you presented this scenario to a group of 5th grade students? How many of them would go up the gangplank from moment one? How many would follow the beckoning welcome of the boney hand? Right – almost all of them.

Why?.. "They don't know any better." Perhaps. "They don't have family responsibilities as we do." Sure. Jennifer James, who presented this scenario suggested a different tack. She asked, "What do those kids have that we don't?" The audience fumbled around with its answers. James sharpened her focus. "Why do these kids not fear the alien, the boney finger from the mist? What somewhat recent media event helped our students to appreciate the universe?" **Voila! E.T.!**

Of course...and Stephen Spielberg's engaging creature, E.T., has given the universe back to our kids. Unlike most adults, our students have a healthy sense of curiosity about the universe. Their patterns of thinking are more open than ours. You may argue that when we were their age, we were raised without the benefit of this delightful alien – the creature who munched Reese's Pieces and waited for a message to call home. Some of us slightly older folks remember the "Creature from the Black Lagoon" – one capable of sucking the brain from the back of your head! A decidedly different image. We were raised on a fear of the unknown – and that sense has remained with us in our adult world.

Consider the spaceship story again – how did you fare? Did you spring up the gangplank, momentarily hold back, or dig in your heels? Your response gives you a glimpse at how you might process new tasks in a conscious fashion. Though the percentages differ in the organization called school, the categories of response ("enthusiastic cheerleaders," "cautious but able Mables," and "no way Jose's") do exist. In order to open our antennae to change we need to better understand ourselves and the habits we perpetuate.

Too often those who encourage change in the schools fail to identify the link between **habit** and the **culture** of the organization. (Culture can be defined simply as "the way we do things around here.") If individual staff members and designated leaders fail to address their personal motives, attitudes, and performance, if it becomes readily apparent that little of substance has actually changed in the way the system functions or how teachers and students behave, then HABIT may be the driving element in the organization.

PROFILE

You may know me.
I'm your constant companion.
I'm your greatest helper,
I'm your heaviest burden.
I will push you onward or
  drag you down to failure.
I am at your command.
Half the tasks you do might as well be
  turned over to me. I'm able to do
  them the same every time if that's
  what you want.
I'm easily managed, all you've got to
  do is see me doing what you want.
Show me exactly how you want it done,
  after a few lessons I'll do it automatically.
I am the servant of all great men and women,
  of course, servant of the failures as well.
I work with all the precision of a marvelous
  computer, with the intelligence of a human.
You may run me for profit or you may run me
  to ruin, it makes no difference to me.
Take charge of me and I'll put the
  world at your feet.
Be easy with me and I will destroy you.
Who am I?

I'm Habit!

Author unknown

Habits positively frame many aspects of our lives. Consciously assessing what we do helps us to break habits that constrict and enables us to lean on those that free us to confront the challenges of life, the challenge of growth, the challenge of change.

One of my favorite assessment tools is to encourage people to examine their seating patterns. To enable people to become more in touch with their habits, they are asked to consciously assess where they sit in the bi-monthly staff meeting, in their traditional row in church or synagogue, or even at the dinner table.

Picture a traditional Thanksgiving meal; think of where Grandmother, the matriarch of the clan, sat, or the youngest child, the parents, other family members, yourself. Pretty clear isn't it? Now think of dinner at your home. You probably have a seating pattern that people automatically utilize. If you are in the minority of American families who still dine together, try this on for size.

Arrive early at the table and purposely sit at a chair other than your own. Watch people's reactions when they arrive. Moving your location breaks familiarity, the order that is a part of everyday living, and upsets people.

A colleague tried that challenge in her home. A family of three: Diane, her engineer husband and their six year old son. Son sat down first in his usual seat. Diane next sat down but in her husband's place. She then called for her husband to join them. He entered the dining area, observed the situation, turned around and left the room. He returned, scratched his head and sat down in the vacant chair. Meanwhile the little guy was laughing. Diane asked him what was so funny and the child said, "It's funny because you are sitting in Daddy's seat!" Even early in life we pattern our behaviors from habit or "the way we do things around here."

Yet changing habits/patterns can create dysfunction and insecurity. Erich Fromm provides additional enlightenment in this area with this statement:

> *The psychic task which a person can and must set for himself is not to feel secure, but to be able to tolerate insecurity.*

From a growth perspective, leaving safe harbors to try short "flights of difference" is important. It helps to keep us sharp, to be able to tolerate insecurities.

BARRIERS TO CHANGE

From an organizational sense, we need to be in touch with the dynamics of change to enhance professional growth possibilities. Organizationally, resistance to change is often a reaction to the methods used in implementing a change.

People view a pattern of leadership and anticipate a certain response. They usually get what they expect. And just as staff members are conditioned by the patterns of their leaders, their response conditions the leader as well. It's circular reinforcement.

Resistance often occurs when people have changes forced upon them or face ones that just don't make sense. If change agents violate habit or the way things are"spozed to be" then they, like my friend's husband at the dinner table, may become disoriented. Even if the change makes sense, or is carefully presented, resistance does occur. This fact ties directly into the notion of habit and is often rooted in perfectionistic control which was discussed in Chapter 3.

How often have we heard the following statements when a new idea was presented?

> *You can do it if you want – but I'm not.*
> *We tried that years ago.*
> *This is impractical.*
> *I don't see anything wrong with what we're doing now.*
> *Our problem is different.*
> *It's almost the same thing as we're doing.*
> *It's too complicated.*
> *Let's be realistic for once.*
> *It's not in the budget.*
> *I think it needs more research.*
> *Here he / she goes again.*
> *It's not our problem, it's the home.*
> *It's too much trouble to make these changes.*
> *We don't have enough time.*
> *The school isn't ready for this.*
> *It looks good on paper but it'll never work.*
> *Sure everything is fine if it works – but what if it bombs?*
> *They won't let us.*
> *We don't have enough authority.*
> *It's a good idea, but...*
> *This too shall pass.*

The last one when translated says... "I can wait this one out, I can outlast the change – this thing doesn't have substance – it **too** shall pass." Sound familiar? No doubt you can come up with your own litany of excuses for standing pat, yet to empower a school we have to be smart enough to get out of the saddle when our horse has died.

Much of the earlier material dealt with strengthening individuals' understanding of change. We now shift to methods for dealing effectively with resistance to change. Understanding and applying these techniques is important to organizational growth. The posture portrayed in Jim Unger's "Herman" has no place in the empowered school.

There are many ways of dealing with resistance to change. EDUCATION and clear COMMUNICATIONS are good on-going approaches. These are essential as you build a foundation for change and keep people in touch about the proposed development. Through education and communication people grow less fearful of it. Once persuaded by the merits of the proposal staff will help implement the change. Open and extensive communication is essential over the long haul – especially in building organizational momentum.

1990 Jim Unger. Reprinted with permission of Universal Press Syndicate. All Rights Reserved.

An involvement/participation approach then expands the organization's leadership base. When those who participate help to shape the plan, shared leadership and ownership result. Their commitment will help insure acceptance of the new approach.

When people resist a change, facilitating the change by greasing the wheels is a helpful technique to use. Evident support by colleagues and administrators of both the resisting individual and the desired change can result in the attitudinal shift desired.

When a group or individual loses face or undergoes adjustments in the conditions of employment, negotiation/agreement becomes a technique organizations employ. Though at times the approach is a relatively easy way to reach consensus, it may not be effective. This is true in a formal negotiations sense if those removed from the change, control the outcome of negotiations. An example of this circumstance might be when a negotiations team of primarily high school personnel, blocks the implementation of a change to interdisciplinary teaming at the middle school because they fear that they might have to follow suit. (This has happened, even though the middle school faculty supported the change.)

One technique that does work but should be used judiciously and with caution is manipulation. It can be a relatively quick and inexpensive solution to some resistance that hasn't yielded to other approaches. The obvious downside of this approach is that when people feel they have been manipulated, resentment occurs. Trust exits the communication process. Manipulation can "deep-six" the change after it has begun and cause people to derail future change initiatives when people recollect how they were used as "pawns."

Coercion is a harsh word, but as a technique it can work. When speed is essential and those who initiate the change have considerable power rapid change can occur. If used often, this approach disempowers the organization and creates a sense of powerlessness in individuals because they haven't influenced or "owned" the change. Use it only as a last resort.

Understanding these approaches and knowing when to utilize them helps leaders to be successful in positively guiding and/or reacting to the change process. Lasting change heavily favors the first three approaches. *Negotiation* is necessary when collective decisions of a formal nature need to be reached. But be particularily wary of *manipulation* and *coercion*, the battle may appear to be won, but at the expense of ultimate victory and lasting change.

Recognizing that change is not only inevitable but is desirable in any healthy organization is important. There are effective ways of dealing with the natural resistance to change through...

Education,
Communication,
Involvement,
Participation,
Facilitation, and
Support.

Thus the question of how we sensitize ourselves to change and gently bring others along with us, becomes pertinent. These verities may help.

CHANGE IS:

- A process not an event
- A highly personal experience
- First made by individuals, then by organizations
- Developmental, involving growth in feelings and skills
- Related to people first and to the change second.

Said simply, don't blow people away with massive change unless major surgery is mandatory. But when an "operation" is called for involve others, help both individuals and groups to confront change through your personal example, your enthusiasm, and through positive communications. Convey the notion that the quest for excellence through change is natural, right, and a reflection of our commitment to improving education for youth.

While change may be uncomfortable, even viewed as a loss by some, and different for each person, it is easier to accept when others are enthusiastic. Leadership that recognizes this reality is more successful in empowering individuals, who then will empower the organization.

Key elements essential to effective change are flexibility, self- esteem, and a sense of humor.

> *Life...*
> *Excellence...*
> *Quality...*
> *Happiness...*
> *Passion...*
>
> *Require*
>
> *A bias for action*
> *An awareness of change, and*
> *The ability to take risks.*

What does the process of change actually entail, what is change all about? When you deal with anything that is different, something that breaks habit, something you haven't tried before, that event may be called a "window of change." It can be simple as brushing your teeth by placing your toothbrush in a different location inside your mouth. (You probably unconsciously brush the same teeth first each morning!) A window of change can be taking a different route home from school, implementing a new reading series, or changing your outward appearance through a new hair style.

Passing through windows of change is a process that we can visualize. It applies to both individuals and groups, teachers and administrators, and occurs in discreet phases:

Exploration
↓
Teetering
↓
Tumbling
↓
Landing
↓
Sharing

Suppose the school is contemplating the implemention of interdisciplinary teaming in the seventh grade. The phases of change could look like this...

Exploration Phase. A representative committee responds to the desire to find out more about teaming. They assign tasks, review the literature, visit neighboring districts, and gather research data.

Teetering Phase. This is where, armed with data, knowing its accuracy, and convinced that teaming is a better approach than that presently used you come up to the window – step forward, step back, step forward, yet still don't commit. You "teeter" because it's tough to break habits and comfortable organizational patterns. But at one of these moments, preferably joined by others and encouraged by leaders, you ultimately plunge through.

Tumbling Phase. Without the benefit of hindsight this can be a frightening time. You've ventured forth from safe harbors, and though bouyed by the companionship of others, the newly accepted concept hasn't yet proven itself. But with time it becomes evident that your decision was right on target, so you land upright, in one piece.

Landing On Your Feet. You are now able to stand tall with the security of knowing your decision was correct because kids are better monitored, parent/staff and staff/staff communications have been greatly improved, and pupil performance has increased. You glow with the pride of accomplishment, and see your pride reflected in your colleagues. You feel great!

Sharing Phase. This is when you have become an "authority," able to share your teaming success story with others. In fact, you do so with such fervor that others wish you would find new windows to approach so you would be less zealous than you are now.

A personal story illustrates how change phases take place in an individual case. A few years ago during a brutally cold western New York winter, I decided to do something for myself. I had been doing what others said was a fine job as a school principal, the job jar around the house wasn't overflowing, and my sons and bride of twenty-seven years were happy. Yet the full schedule I was keeping during the week was such that I rarely made it past half-time of a Sunday T.V. Buffalo Bills game before I drifted off. I also noticed my pants seemed to have shrunk around the waist.

So characteristically of my compulsive nature, I decided to go on a physical fitness routine. I scanned my options (**exploration phase**) and decided to jog. Yet when it came down to it, I wasn't sure that this activity was appropriate. Though my boyhood track experience was a distant memory, my recollection was that I enjoyed running. That was a plus. But the temperature was ten degrees below zero – a *decided* minus. What to do? (**teetering phase**). I decided to go for it. Through the window I tumbled.

So into the cold, dressed like a yeti monster (the abominable snowman) went Joseph – face mask, blue parka, ski gloves, woolies and my old basketball sneakers moving in what must have appeared as a middle aged mud slide oozing around the blocks of our community. My ever-stylish family disowned me; my wife's suspicions about my mental state were confirmed – but jog I did.

When I first began my slothful movement through the neighborhood, every pore of my body was screaming for mercy. Though my mind told me that this routine was good for me, my body was in revolt and wanted to excommunicate the brain from the system. I hurt and was unsure of the wisdom of my decision. (**tumbling phase**) Yet perserverance is my trademark so perservere I did.

A warming trend hit the second week, the temperature climbed to zero. Things were getting better, I was feeling better. I had lost some weight, and neighbors no longer ran to the window to laugh at the blue barge charging around the streets.

In fact, every day I was feeling better and better. About the third week, I even went out and purchased a better pair of running shoes. In terms of the change process, I had tumbled through the window and had landed on my feet. (**landing**)

At work people hid from me because they knew that I would wax on the virtues of running. (**sharing**) Even though the temperature hovered around zero, things were going great. Roger Bannister move over.

Somewhere around the fourth week a friend sent me an article from the *New England Journal of Medicine*...on penile frost bite! I took up swimming the next day!!

A true story – one that effectively illustrates both the phases and the change process that I personally experienced.

An additional phase is **adjustment**. If new data revises questions about the validity of your change, explore new windows and adjust. When someone who understands the concept of windows and change is confident, it is fairly easy to adjust. Even though one's motivation may not be strong, modification and adjustments may be made at any point. Remember that change for the sake of change isn't valid, but change for improvement is a healthy aspect of empowered schools.

If you think change is scary, **risk** can be downright intimidating. Yet risk can be managed nicely if it is taken in very tiny steps. Once you have an awareness of the need to take a risk, taking small bites of a big problem will produce results.

Consider this illustration. If at the first meeting of the year the brand new principal were to say..."Our format for today is to have the staff break into discussion groups to dialog on four specific problem areas. Discuss them for the next 40 minutes and give me proposed resolutions of the problems by the time you leave today."

Picture that staff, especially if their previous "designated leader" read memos to them at their monthly get togethers. The new principal would be moving to an advanced point before she had walked the staff through any preliminary steps. Establishing gradual yet clearly identifiable phases would have helped bring staff along. And to help them embrace the change, they had to actively participate in staff meetings and decisions prior to implementing them full tilt. The principal's risk in varying the format was well intentioned, but the process was counter-productive.

A series of questions that one might ask oneself when facing a new challenge and about to risk is:

- What good things will happen if I do this?
- What's the worst thing that can happen if I do this?
- What is most likely to happen if I do this?
- Do the benefits outweigh the negatives?
- Will what I want to accomplish survive the worst case scenerio?
- Will *I* survive the worst case scenerio?

If both you and your objective can survive the worst then you have nothing to fear – so go for it! As with change, there is a process of risk. It looks like this...

- Recognizing the need
- Deciding to risk
- Making the commitment
- Reaching the point of no return
- Completing the risk
- Adapting to it
- Evaluating your actions

Here's an illustration. Several years ago I was driving to a school district in New York to conduct a workshop. I was running a bit late and needed to pick up my pace. On a two lane rural road I found myself following a slow-moving tractor trailer. I realized that unless I passed the truck my chances of being on time would diminish. (Recognizing the need) What to do? I decided to pass the truck

Our children often handle change better than their teachers.
We need to follow their lead.

in a safe passing zone (Decided to risk) and chose what appeared to be a good place and hit the accelerator. (Making the commitment) About halfway (Reaching the point of no return) I saw that coming in the other direction was the big brother of the truck I was passing.

What now? Jam on my brakes and hope the truck I was passing maintained its speed? Drive off the road and risk an accident? Accelerate? I sped up, safely passed the truck and pulled back into my lane with relief. (Completed the risk) I reduced my speed (Adapted) and asked myself... "Was it worth it?" (Evaluation) The answer was, "no way!"

Risk is a process. Change is a process. Growth is a process. A process of moving forward, of testing, of experiencing, and of evaluation. We sort from our experience in order to grow. The empowered organization **risks** opportunities for growth. The greater the change the more we must avoid superficial thought and undisciplined good intentions. Analysis is essential. In the next chapter we will deal with three A's – *assessment*, *analysis* and *action*. Effective change in the empowered school must deal with all three. 🍎

Chapter 5

Assessment, Analysis, Action:
The 3 "A's" of the Empowered School

"Would you tell me, please," said Alice, "which way I ought to go from here?"

"That depends a good deal on where you want to get to," said the Cat.

"I don't much care where," said Alice.

"Then it doesn't matter which way you go," said the Cat.

"– so long as I get somewhere," Alice added as an explanation.

"Oh, you're sure to do that," said the Cat, "if you only walk long enough."

– Lewis Carroll

Knowing where one is heading makes obvious sense, but, like Alice, many schools exist in a "Wonderland" without clear direction and focus. Knowing where you are heading enables you to determine the best route to take in order to get there. Taking stock of your talents helps to determine the means you have available to use in reaching your destination.

ANALYSIS is critical also, but at times it can be overdone. Take for example the bumblebee. Scientists can prove that it is aerodynamically impossible for the bumblebee to fly. Its body is far too heavy for its frail wings to sustain flight. Since the bumblebee chooses not to be influenced by this sophisticated analysis, it flies, works, contributes and finds time each day to make a little honey.

In a sense we need to be like the bumblebee – capable beyond apparent limitations and openly analyze our procedures and patterns in order to improve.

Ulysses S. Grant, nearing his death, wrote a letter to his physician. It was a personal statement; a retrospective that helped to define his existence:

The fact is that I think that I am a verb instead of a personal pronoun. A verb is anything that signifies to be, to do, or to suffer. I signify all three.

91

What Grant said is essentially true of organizations for it is only when we are like an action verb that we find focus. Only when we know who we are; only when we reflect on what we are doing; and only when we match our actions to a desired set of objectives, do we succeed in creating empowered schools. This process is the substance of this chapter.

In a meeting the total school staff was analyzing the year to see if our behaviors had been congruent with our objectives. Healthy sub-group discussions occurred and a number of ideas were generated that might fine-tune our efforts.

The next day a relatively new faculty member who was an excellent physical education teacher, came to see me. The following conversation ensued.

"Joe, I've been thinking about yesterday's meeting and I believe we've got a problem."

"Tell me more, Jack. If you've identified a concern, let's see if we can't resolve it."

"The problem is with detention. It appears that we've been assigning students to after-school detention if they haven't suited up for gym class."

"On the surface that seems to be okay, Jack. If students have not chosen to be responsible by being prepared for class, then an after school make-up class is a logical consequence."

"That's not the problem. It's what we've been doing," elaborated Jack. "Our practice has been to apply the curriculum as a punishment." He noticed my confused look and continued, "We've been having kids run laps and do calisthenics as a punitive consequence during their after school time."

The light clicked on for me. "Ah...it's like the English teacher who has difficulty with a talkative student who constantly disrupts the lesson – who then assigns the youngster a 500 word composition on 'Why I shouldn't talk out in class'. The kid may talk less in class but learns to hate writing."

"Exactly, and calisthenics are an integral part of the wellness curriculum that I want my students to pursue and enjoy. So, I've got a plan – and I think it's a pretty good one. Let me run it by you." Jack replied eagerly.

Jack then explained his plan which he subsequently put into operation. Next Wednesday, 18 seventh and eighth grade students showed up for after-school gym. These girls hadn't suited up for their regular P.E. class and had "earned" the make-up session after school that day.

 As the students gathered around the teacher, one said: "What are we going to do today Mr. Mertel? Run laps, do jumping jacks, push-ups?"

"The first thing you are going to do," said the teacher, "is to go into that locker room and change into your gym clothes!"

"Okay," said the students as they scooted to the locker room.

Quickly they re-assembled, all dressed in their P.E. clothes. One youngster queried, "What are we gonna do now, Mr. Mertel, chin ups, squat thrusts?"

"You know kids, for the first time in my life I made a mistake. What I really want you to do is to go back into that locker room and change back into your school clothes."

"Okay," said the students as they dutifully filed back into the locker room. Returning they asked, "What do you want us to do now, Mr. Mertel?"

"Kids," said Jack, "you may find this hard to believe, but for the second time in my life, I made a mistake. What I'd really like you to do is go back into that locker room and change into your gym clothes!"

"Okay," said the kids and off they went, willingly but wondering. Upon their return one student said, "What are we gonna do now, Mr. Mertel, stretching exercises, lift weights or are you going to make us change again?!"

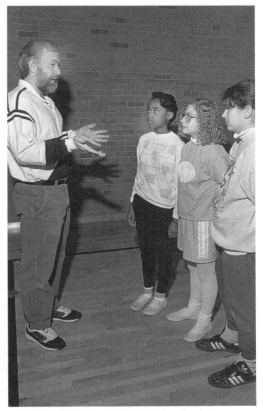

An unorthodox but effective technique used by a physical education teacher.

"Precisely," said Jack, **"because that's the skill that you need to work on and that's the reason why you're here today!"**

Those kids sure got a lot of practice changing clothes that day. After twenty-two changes in their hour and fifteen minutes of detention, the kids dragged out for dismissal. The little sharpie who had first figured out the afternoon agenda said:

"Mr. Mertel, I want you to know a few things! First, I'm never going to be unprepared for gym class again. Furthermore I'm going to tell all my friends that you're crazy. And, I'm going to tell them that they had better suit up for gym class, too!"

What Jack accomplished was to have his students deal with the causal factor that resulted in their assignment to an after school make-up class. He did not "punish" students using the very elements which he wanted them to value as they developed an overall attitude of physical wellness. This was a classic case on letting the punishment fit the crime.

It is now extremely rare to see any youngster in our school unprepared for gym class. We have a superb physical education staff and curriculum but, I suspect, part of the reason for the success is the manner in which Jack *assessed, analyzed* and *acted* in modifying a problem that had been unconsciously perpetuated for years.

Open-ended group thinking can release the individual talents of an organization, whereas restrictive patterns of thought suppress the basic attitude necessary to effectively assess, analyze and act. A story about the evils of conditioning people's behavior (and tracking as well) goes like this:

Suppose you trapped a number of fleas and kept them captive in a restrictive space. As you know fleas can jump tremendous distances. But, if you take the insects and put them in a jar and put the top on it, the fleas will continuously jump and hit the lid in an attempt to gain their freedom. After a while the fleas will jump no higher than just below the level of the lid. It's not that these insects can't jump higher, it's that they have "learned" not to. In fact, were you to remove the lid, the fleas would continue to jump to a level *below where the lid had been.*

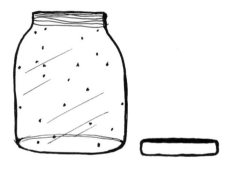

Even though the fleas were motivated to gain their freedom, their restrictive pattern of learning established "caps" on how far they believed they could go – learned helplessness. Organizations limit themselves when thinking becomes restrictive. In the case of fleas, their greatest barrier to what they wanted to achieve, their freedom, was their conditioning.

The flea anecdote sets the stage for an *analysis* of *motivation* in an empowered school.

MOTIVATION

It has been argued correctly that you cannot motivate people. Motivation is inherent in the individual so all you can do is create an environment which is aligned with people's motivation. All people seek to achieve their own objectives, but those objectives are not necessarily *your* objectives *for them*.

The degree to which a school may become empowered is determined by the degree that people share a common vision and move in a manner that is consistent with that goal. That's the key, people's actions or behaviors are targeted to common outcomes. In many organizations commonality is ill defined or ignored. What is the situation in your school?

Scrutinizing the topic of motivation is important to individual and group growth. "What happens in our school?" is an important question. "What understandings about motivation should we use as reference points in order to grow?" is an equally important query. Attention to this topic is important to maximizing individuals' contributions to our organizations.

You are challenged to assess the following points for their applicability to your personal and professional functioning, beginning with an analysis of two diagrams.

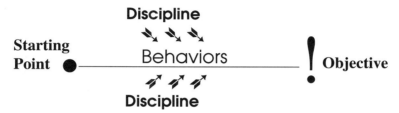

In this diagram, behavior is depicted as a straight line to the goal. Rarely does such on-task behavior occur in its purest sense, but it does occur with greater frequency for individuals who are goal-oriented and are a part of an effective organization. An example may be helpful.

If my objective was to clean out the garage last Saturday and I got up bright and early to do so...and the weather wasn't too nice ...and if my golf clubs remained in the bag...and if a friend didn't call me to go fishing...or if my wife hadn't other plans that were more pressing than mine...then my behavior would be congruent with my objective and I'd clean up the garage. If my discipline was strong, and even if the variables (nice day, fishing trip, etc.) presented alternatives, then I would finish my task.

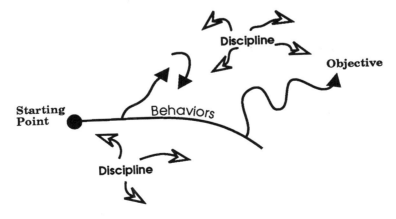

Now in the above diagram even though my objective remains the same – to clean out the garage – my observed behavior wouldn't indicate that this was the case. My *discipline* was weak. This scenario goes like this.

I awake to a beautiful Saturday with the objective of cleaning out the garage. Nine holes of golf later I return home. Peg is planting flowers and I join her. Later we enjoy lunch overlooking the garden. We take a walk, bump into some neighbors and decide to have a cookout, and enjoy each others' company for the evening. My objective was to clean out the garage, but I certainly didn't achieve it. Like the needle on an erratically functioning compass, I pointed everywhere. I took numerous side trips and never fulfilled my original objective.

Behaviors or *actions* must be congruent with *objectives*. If you truly desire to attain them, then both personal motivation and discipline are essential. However, it is not enough to simply *want* to do something. If you really wanted to fly, standing in one place and flapping your arms wouldn't do it. You would exhaust your energy and look mighty foolish in the process. And how you look is a powerful motivator in organizations; because most ***people value more how they appear rather than the substance of what they are.***

This latter point warrants embellishing. Organizationally, we create a climate that subjugates individuality to the prevailing form of the majority. It's called, **the way we do things around here.** The IBM dress code, common time schedules, etc. are organizational ways of life. We need to be sensitive to that reality and recognize that while consistency may support organizational effectiveness, mindless conformity supports the slow decay of organizational thought, creativity, and challenge. What the organization says in its unwritten code drives the individual to come to grips with choices. The enigma is to either conform and give up a degree of uniqueness, or to be a non-conformist and run the risk of being rejected or stalemated in organizational effectiveness and status.

Denis Waitley (1980) developed an interesting theme which applies. He said...

> *Since we always move in the direction of what we are thinking of most, it is imperative to concentrate our thoughts on the conditions we want to achieve rather than try to move away from what we fear or don't want.*

In an instructional tape on self-esteem, Waitley, an advisor to the American Women's Olympic Volleyball Team, recalled the time that he went to observe his daughter's high school team practice. What he observed concerned him greatly. The coach, a seasoned veteran, kept exhorting his players, "Don't let the ball hit the ground, don't let the ball hit the ground!" The ball kept hitting the ground.

What the coach was focusing his players attention on was...the ball **hitting the ground!** Waitley said that this approach was counter-productive. The coach should have said, **"Keep the ball in the air; keep the ball in the air!"**

Imaging is important in the training of athletes. Had the coach focused his player's attention on the ball being in the air, the player's image and subconscious motivation would have increased their ability to do so.

In my judgment one of the most misguided campaigns was the "Just say no!" approach to substance abuse. Using Waitley's logic, what would repeating "Just say no" do? Though the jury is still out on the value of this program just saying "No" concentrates people's attention on **taking drugs**. "Just say no" is a counter productive way of looking at behavior.

In organizations we tend to embellish traps, problems, and the flaws in our functioning. Subsequently we get back what we give. We need to be conscious of this negative human inclination. Negatives beget negatives. A problem or crisis mentality begets problems and crises. We need to counteract this repressive thinking by focusing on the positive outcomes we wish to attain. We need to do this in both our personal lives and our organizations. Sometimes we feel trapped by the prevailing current of negative thinking around us. Keep in mind the following examples if you find yourself "out-gunned" in the future.

Harold Hodgkinson's *Fearless Forecasts* (1985) illustrate how negative thinking can suppress thought...

1865 BOSTON POST
Well-informed people know it is impossible to transmit the voice over wires, and were it possible, the thing would be of no practical value.

1899 CHARLES DUELL, Director of the U.S. Patent Office
Everything that can be invented, has been invented.

1929 DEPARTMENT OF LABOR, Forecast of December 1929
1930 will be a splendid employment year.

1949 POPULAR MECHANICS MAGAZINE
Computers of the future may have only 1,000 vacuum tubes and weigh as little as 1 1/2 tons!

and one that I personally heard shortly after I began my educational service...

1963 NEW YORK STATE EDUCATION DEPARTMENT
Bureau Chief
The middle school concept is a fad – one that will pass from view within the next 5 years!

Obviously these predictions were frightful in their ignorance. But for many they no doubt established the suspicion that their own differing opinion may not have been valid. After all, these were **experts** who were forecasting. Thankfully not all followed the prognostications of the authorities. Keep that in mind when you face all-knowing people in the future.

You probably recall the Mendelian genetic pea experiments studied in your Biology 101 course. The matrix Mendel used to chart the dominance of characteristics is something that can be adapted to provide a unique insight into human motivation.

TASK OUTCOME

	success	failure
SUCCESS	Ss #1	Sf #2
FAILURE	Fs #3	Ff #4

How the Individual Views His/Her Capabilites

The vertical column **S**uccess and **F**ailure represents how an individual views him/herself. The horizontal column represents the actual **s**uccess or **f**ailure of that individual on a specific accomplishment or task. Thus someone in Quadrant #1 *views* himself as a **S**uccess who has **s**uccessfully completed a task. Quadrant #2...The **S**uccess who **f**ails at a task. Quadrant #3...A **F**ailure who **s**ucceeds at a task. Quadrant #4...the person who views himself as a **F**ailure who **f**ails at a task. Okay? Then try these questions.

1. **In which quadrant (#1, #2, #3, #4) might an individual find the greatest degree of pressure? Why?**
2. **In which quadrant might an individual find the least amount of pressure? Why?**
3. **As educators and leaders, what is our major responsibility regarding the motivation of students and colleagues?**
4. **What are two specific things that would help you implement this responsibility?**

Before considering your responses, read this hypothetical situation.

Suppose on a Sunday outing to Rich Stadium in Buffalo to watch the Bills take on the Dallas Cowboys, the Bills' starting quarterback is injured. He's carried off the field just as the Bills punt the ball to the Cowboys on the last play of the series. The back-up quarterback is seen hurriedly warming up on the sidelines in anticipation of entering the game. But he slips on a piece of equipment, twists his ankle, and the doctor won't clear him for playing. The coach has to find a quarterback quickly and turns to the crowd. (Here's where we really stretch this story.) He spots this one guy who may have played the game a few years back and says, "Hoff, suit up, you're going in as Q.B.!" My reaction, no doubt like yours, would be:

"Yeah, sure!"

"Seriously, Hoff, suit up...we need you!" said the team scout.

Still no movement from the fan, the coach says:

"Suit up Hoff, we'll pay you $20,000."

"Where's the locker room? I'm yours!"

Now lest the lunacy of this scenario has yet to hit you, Joe Hoff, former 155 pound track and basketball player at the most basic level of high school competition has just been invited to play on one of the top teams in professional football. Filthy luchre has drawn him into a suicidal role. Aside from the big payday, how does Joe Hoff view himself as a pro football player? (Think of the matrix.)

Correct, a Failure. And what does he expect to do? Correct again, fail Therefore, in what quadrant would he project himself? Obviously, in Quadrant #4, Ff.

Let's continue. Hoff takes the field. The score is tied. There are two minutes left in the game. Buffalo is on their own 15 yard line, 85 yards to go for a score. It's an obvious passing down. Hoff bends over center and takes the snap. He fades back and is provided great protection, throws a pass – smack into the derriere of his own offensive lineman!

What has Hoff, the one who viewed himself as a Failure, done? Yup, he's failed. And what does Hoff feel like? Correct "I told you so." Does he feel good? NO. Does he feel as if he should be on the field with this great team? NO again. "What did you expect anyhow?" he says.

Let's change the scenario.

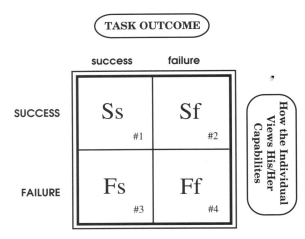

Two minutes left in the game. The ball is on the Buffalo 15. Hoff fades back and throws a pass. Somehow the ball floats over the on-rushing Dallas linemen, the defender slips, Andre Reed, the wideout for Buffalo, makes a spectacular grab of this wounded duck and sprints toward the end zone. Reed crosses midfield, just one man to beat, 40, 30, 20, 10, 5 **TOUCHDOWN**. Buffalo wins the game. Hoff has thrown the winning pass!

In what quadrant does Hoff now place himself? Of course: Fs – the Failure has succeeded. What does Hoff feel? He is absolutely shocked about his success. Does he feel he's ready to compete for Jim Kelly's job? Definitely not. Does he feel he's capable of doing it again? Definitely not.

And this is where the essence of MOTIVATION lies – it takes *multiple successes* for those who view themselves as failures or those whom others have so conditioned to feel that they are anything but a failure.

Let's switch gears. Two minutes left in the game, Hoff is where he belongs—in the stands. Jim Kelly, the quarterback, has recovered from his injury and returns to the game. 85 yards to go for a score. Kelly, fades back and throws a pass, incomplete. In what quadrant do we place this all-pro, top notch quarterback after this play? Right! Quadrant #2, Sf. The Success has failed. What does Kelly feel? It steels his resolve.

He fades back, throws another pass – another incompletion. This time it was dropped by a wide open Bills player who could have scored had he held on to the ball. Same quadrant...what does he feel? Does he jump all over the player who dropped the ball. No way. He is a leader and motivator of others. "Let's get 'em this time!"

Kelly fades back, Reed breaks into the clear, Kelly throws a perfect pass, Reed catches the ball, eludes two defenders and cruises into the end zone for the winning score. What does Kelly feel? Elation! Is he shocked as Hoff was in this same scenario? No. He knew as a Success (Ss) that he would succeed. And he did.

Now you might want to rethink your previous answers to questions #1 and #2. The correct response, based on motivational theory, follows.

Question #1 - In what quadrant might an individual find the greatest degree of pressure?

Most people respond that it is in the Ss, Quadrant #1 or Sf, Quadrant #2 boxes. Not true. The greatest degree of pressure was not to have the Success succeed (#1) but in the Failure, fails quadrant (#4).

These individuals are dysfunctional. These individuals are at risk, and though they may put up what I refer to as a wall of Jello (press here and I'll bounce back over there, you can't reach me), their pain is real and deep, and inside. They feel tremendous pressure but can't or won't show it.

The **second question** follows this logic closely – **Where is the least amount of pressure found?** The individual in the first quadrant (Ss) feels the least amount of pressure. From a psychological perspective, people who view themselves as successes who succeed, have realized once again what they feel deep down inside, "I'm good stuff and I have it". Their centering is confidence and it enables the Successes to have a strong "self-speak" attitude and a positive momentum even in the face of a temporary setback.

Let's hold on the reaction to questions #3 and #4 for a moment.

Organizations that have a pattern of negative "self-speak" drive themselves in the direction of their dominant thinking. The staff meeting gripe session sets the tone for more of the same and depresses the participants. A parent conference that begins with teachers presenting a litany of failing grades and/ or an accounting of behavioral problems created by the student, frames negatives that cause the parent to shut down the listening that must be present if a coalition of improvement is to be formed.

The Ss organization deals with its glitches but does not become preoccupied with a form of negativism. The organization that identifies areas where improvement is needed, brainstorms positive alternatives, and then implements wise choices, is going to ride the crest of success for a long time.

The parent conference that begins with some positive validation of the student and seeks to establish common purposes will effectively address improvement strategies.

Now return to questions #3 and #4.

Question #3 - As educators, what is our major responsibility regarding the motivation of our students and colleagues?

It is our challenge to take those who perceive themselves as failures and provide consistent, incremental opportunities for success. Success breeds success. When people develop a sense that they can succeed, they will. If they "image" success, have incentives to achieve, and are reinforced when successes do occur, the pattern and feelings of failure will be reversed.

Accordingly, we need to program opportunities for success into our classrooms, staff interactions, meetings, and organizational thinking. Those who succeed cast a light of accomplishment to others. Our task is to take this light and spread opportunities for all to succeed. In other words, we need to provide:

• A nurturing environment with abundant success opportunities, especially for those who travel the longest road home (Ff).

• Challenge and revalidation for those whose successes and focus may be clear, so that they may be externally rewarded or validated by colleagues and classmates. In that manner each may be internally rewarded or valued by him/herself. Confidence is necessary for individual and organizational growth, and to encourage movement from failure to success quadrants.

Question #4 - What are two specific things that would help you implement this responsibility?

Suggestion #1 **- Understand and use reinforcers to increase individual and organizational success.**

Some informational thoughts on reinforcement –

• *Receiving positive strokes or consequences for a certain behavior results in an increase in that behavior.* Fundamentally this is what reinforcement is all about.

• *Reinforcement is a major tool for supporting change in individuals and groups.*

The two basic ways of reinforcing people are to –
   1. give them something they desire or like
   2. remove something that they dislike or don't want

Some process thoughts on reinforcing –

• *When using reinforcement, personalize it.* People relate to people. Therefore, don't be afraid to use the "I" word. "I really appreciate your willingness to _____. It resulted in _____."

• *When you reinforce several people* (for the same task, success, contributions) *use personal names and vary your letters.* Identical memos give an impersonal feeling. Make it special. They are, so recognize and say it.

• *Sooner is better than later when you reinforce.* Feedback immediately after the behavior links the consequence with the action and strengthens the behavior *especially* when one moves away from the failure/failure quadrant. These folks have to believe that they can. Extrinsic reinforcers are psychological cues to enhance internal confidence and internal confidence expands one's own personal motivation.

• *Be cautious about the frequency of reinforcement.* Too much reinforcement may set up a dependency relationship. Yet more is better than less when administered directly after desired behavior. Consistent reinforcement at the onset of an attitude or quadrant shift (Ff to Fs, or Fs to Ss) is highly important. A parallel example is when we use massed practice to reinforce a learned concept. Initially more is desirable, eventually periodic reinforcement takes over.

• As a reinforcer, be sensitive to your objective in administering the reinforcement. An increase of the desired behavior, such as the student's or colleague's confidence enhancement, is the goal. As flattering as it may seem, their dependence on you is not the desired outcome. Remember that weaning others from your leadership enables them to develop their own ability to lead. Kahlil Gibran in his classic, *The Prophet,* shared his thoughts on teaching:

> *If he (the teacher) is indeed wise he does not bid you to enter the house of his wisdom, but rather leads you to the threshold of your own mind.*

The degree of success that individuals or organizations achieve is directly proportional to the belief that the individuals or organizations have relative to success. The staff must believe that the workplace has more consequences of a positive than negative nature. The organizational culture and management need to provide them. Reinforcement theory indicates that at least four positive reinforcers for every negative will encourage goal-centered behavior within the organization. Most administrators work from a 2:1 ratio. Many do little or nothing of a positive nature in proximity to the performance of the desired behavior yet, that is the time when reinforcers work best.

We need to be aware that *doing nothing is doing something.* When one ignores poor performance, poor performance is perpetuated. When someone breaks a pattern and meets with a success, doing nothing leaves the behavior isolated and out on a limb.

Not complimenting a well-cooked meal says to the chef that you didn't like it. The likelihood of seeing that meal again or the effort that went into it is diminished. Pro-actively doing something is more often than not a far better choice than doing nothing.

Sincere reinforcement brings results. Varying your approach keeps your actions fresh, both for the recipient and yourself. Avoid the canned response at all costs. Specific reinforcement drives behavior in a desired direction. "Playing back" what people did lets them know what you specifically find of value.

Our emphasis in organizations is to increase productivity, harmony, and goal attainment. Positive reinforcement is one of the most effective means of having employees achieve work-related goals.

Positive reinforcement increases the performance you want and has other desirable side effects. Relationships between designated leaders and staff improve. Individuals are liked more. Job satisfaction increases. The job is more satisfying. Morale improves. The organization is liked more. Positive reinforcement encourages people to do more in the specific areas you help them to target.

Suggestion #2 - Develop and use a system that validates/reinforces people quickly, effectively, and enthusiastically.

~~~~~~~~~~~~~~~~~~~

Thought You Ought to Know

YOU GOT CAUGHT
DOING THE NEATEST THING...

I admire your obvious interest in professional growth. As you consciously reinforce the many positives of your students and colleagues, their successes will increase even more. Thanks for taking an active interest in this section of our book.

AND I KNOW BECAUSE I
WAS THERE!

Joseph W. Hoff

~~~~~~~~~~~~~~~~~~~

Recognition, praise, and positive reinforcement are essential to individual and organizational productivity and morale. A study conducted by Motivational Systems (1988), a management development company, indicated that as many as 25,000,000 American workers would quit their jobs were another job a possibility because they believed they weren't appreciated. Thirty-eight percent of those surveyed felt their bosses left them to function in isolation without appreciation, recognition, or praise for their performance. Many managers mistakenly assume that salary is the solitary incentive and motivator. It's not.

Motivational praise (reinforcement), the correct use of it requires:

CONSISTENCY. Immediate, enthusiastic, sincere recognition as close to the desired behavior as possible.

SPECIFICITY. The person needs to know exactly what behavior you are praising.

ELABORATION. Explain the benefits of the behavior and the positive impact it has had, wherever possible.

FUTURE AWARENESS. The key is continuous growth. Individuals are encouraged to continue positive behavior as a benchmark for continued success. Helping people to confidently engage their own motivators and to broaden them is inherent in an empowered organization. It results in personal and professional job satisfaction. This enlarged perspective is extremely important in assessing what you are doing.

The key question is, **Why are you doing what you are doing?** There is more substance to this inquiry than immediately meets the eye, just as the following story will illustrate.

The Fable of the Frog, the Fisherman, and the Snake

Conrad was a hard working dedicated educator who gave his all to his students and his job. Though the pressures of his work were great he had found a way to release tension and find peace in his life. Each Saturday at the crack of dawn on a small farm pond, Conrad could be found in a small aluminum boat with a big straw hat, a cane pole with a bobber, drifting lazily in the gentle tranquil retreat. Sometimes he would put a hook and a worm on the line , sometimes not. It was the serenity and solitude that he sought.

Now even though pretty much a teetotaler, Conrad was said to partake of some liquid spirits in these moments of reverie. One particularly beautiful morning as steam rose skyward from the glassy pond, Conrad had just finished his lunch (7:00 am) and settled back blissfully sipping from a flask of Jim Beam.

All of a sudden – great splashing startled our hero. Carefully putting down his libation, he surveyed the scene – and there within arm's reach of the boat was this fierce water snake whose jaws contained this adorable, itty bitty, tiny green frog. Now being a man of action, Conrad bent over in an instant scooping up the snake – careful not to tempt the fangs of this viper. He picked up a small stick and delicately wedged it into the snake's mouth just enough so that the adorable, itty bitty, tiny green frog could escape to the safety of the waters.

Holding the snake, Conrad realized that he had just deprived one of God's creatures of its' normal food source. He looked 'round the boat. What to give it...alas, he had finished the meal his wife had packed for him. Ah, of course! Conrad picked up the flask and poured a healthy amount into the snake's gullet. He once again put down the flask and removed the stick from the viper's mouth. Carefully he returned the snake to the waters and watched it swim away.

Anxious to regain the tranquility of his hideaway, Conrad picked up his flask, leaned back when all of a sudden be heard...Bam! Bam! Bam! on the side of the boat! Startled he looked down and saw that same snake **with two frogs in his mouth!**

Many organizations have conflicted value systems. We hope for behavior "A", reward behavior "B" and then wonder why we don't get the behavior we desire. As with the *Frog, The Fisherman, and the Snake*, we get more of the behavior we reward. Come what may, people will do the things that reward them the most. As an example, consider one common use of the public address system. End of day announcements include information about after-school activities, upcoming events, mini-sermons from the administration and...

"Will the following students report for after school detention in room 106. Rose Swiskey, Gwen Papania, Sandy McCauley, Ron Vitale, Don Seidel, Gladys Beisman, Colleen Currie, Julia Hahn, John DeBaun, Barbara Johnson, Eileen Kelly and George Hoff." What does this practice do? Of course, it gives this distinguished crew an Andy Warholian quarter hour of fame, notoriety, and prominence, a time in the sun. This misuse of the P.A. system has elevated the student's inappropriate behavior, put it in lights so to speak, and has given attention to the very behavior we do not wish to encourage. That's what is meant when I said we reward behavior "B" yet wonder why we don't get more of behavior "A". In trying to do the right thing, we often fall into the trap of rewarding the wrong activities and ignoring the right ones.

Prominent "lecher," General Halftrack, surely exemplifies this point.

Though the work of Michael LeBoeuf on organizational rewards is in the business world, direct inferences for schools can be drawn from his research *(Greatest Management Principle in the World, 1985).* Synthesizing his studies, one may conclude that the single most important key to improving organizations is establishing the proper link between performance and rewards. Reward people for the right behavior and you get the right results.

The staff and I extend our
sincere congratulations to you
for your selection as an honor student
at Churchville-Chili Middle School

Your continued efforts and positive attitude will bring success
to you and pride to your family in the future.

Sincerely,

Joseph W. Hoff
Principal

Mailed to students who earn designation as an honors student, this card has been extremely well received.

LeBoeuf's line of questioning in **The 10 Most Frequent Mistakes Made On The Job,** is particularly pertinent. See how many of them you may have either observed or heard about.

Do we...

• need better results, but reward those who look busiest?

• ask for quality work, but set unreasonable deadlines?

• want solid solutions to problems, but reward quick fixes?

• talk about loyalty, but provide questionable security?

• need simplicity, but reward those who complicate matters and generate trivia?

• ask for a harmonious work climate, but reward squeaky wheels who complain the most?

• need creative employees, but chastise those who dare to be different?

• talk about frugality, but award the largest budget increases to those who exhaust all of their budgets?

• ask for teamwork, but reward one team member at the expense of another?

• need self-starters, but penalize unsuccessful risk-takers?

These probing and disturbing questions need to be addressed. Though targeted to private sector business, an analysis of your school could very well deal with these issues as well.

If the following practices are being conducted in your school, as they are in many schools across our nation, then your assessment and analysis will lead to actions that will redress these wrongs.

The Reward Systems of Schools Are Often Confused

WE SPOTLIGHT POOR BEHAVIOR...

As in the P.A. system example, we often highlight improprieties in school. Negative messages and poorly stated rules are prominently displayed. Remember Waitley's logic about being driven in the direction we think of most? In one school there were negative messages all over the place. "No running in the halls." "Don't throw food in the cafeteria." They even had a time clock for the entire staff to punch. The place reeked of negativism and a lack of trust. As you might suspect, discipline, and the instructional outcomes were poor.

To correct those conditions it was necessary to establish a dialogue about what the various practices/procedures were doing to the *culture* of the school. By holding a mirror for people to look into resulted in some significantly different approaches to the sharing of rules with students. Highlighting positive behavior begets more of the same. The converse is also very true as our colleagues in that school readily discovered – and changed.

WE SHOWCASE WINNING EXCLUSIVELY RATHER THAN
HIGHLIGHTING ATTITUDE AND PARTICIPATION...

Walk into the lobby of any secondary school and what do you see? **The trophy case!** Sports accomplishments may be one of the jewels in a school's crown, but should we thus highlight those who have excelled in athletics to the exclusion of others? Why not highlight students of the month who reached success yet who presently bask in their own anonymity? What about the kids who shine in the face of adversity? Who contribute to the harmony and effectiveness of their classmates, school, and teachers? They deserve a place of honor as well.

WE FAIL TO DEVELOP GROUP ACCOUNTABILITY AND PEER CONTROLS...

Belonging to something larger than ourselves is a hallmark of effective organizations. Team identity is woven into the fabric of the empowered school. When individuals both influence the group's actions and are influenced by the group's actions, corporate responsibility develops.

Various research studies *(e.g. Osgood, 1980)* indicate that **five elements of success in business** are:

- innovation
- fast moving flexibility
- goal directed competitiveness; competition/ improvement within oneself versus competition with other people
- shared decision making/decisiveness
- being a team player

The latter two elements underscore the need for group identity. No person is an island unto himself. That thought is particularly salient in today's interdependent society.

WE CRITICIZE THE INDIVIDUAL RATHER THAN THE BEHAVIOR...

Effective organizations value the individual, support the integrity of team members, yet work conscientiously to rectify problems.   When an individual makes a poor choice, members of these organizations collaborate to resolve the problem not condemn the individual.

Picking up the pieces from a risk that hasn't worked out and redirecting the poor behavior of students without destroying their validity or individual worth are essential actions. Often we attack the individual rather than look for ways to correct the errant behavior. If we invalidate the individual's worth, then we establish an expectation that that is the only type of behavior we expect of that person. We stereotype people when we attack them. If the manner in which we approach the individual involves negative expectations, then more often than not, negative behavior is what we get!

WE FAIL TO PROVIDE OPPORTUNITIES FOR CHOICE WITHIN CLEARLY DEFINED BOUNDARIES...

Defining parameters gives people secure boundaries within which people may make choices. Organizations run into problems when roles are poorly defined. Schools need to set secure boundaries and have a range of choice within those boundaries. Rewarding initiative, sharing decisions, and sharing a purpose, lead to ownership and shared successes. These are all aspects of a healthy organization.

From a psychological perspective four of the elements that contribute to **organizational well-being** are:

1. Doing something important
2. Involvement
3. A degree of independence
4. Having a sense of control of one's destiny

These four items have a direct linkage to **CHOICE** within the organization. Choosing to be powerful (a major element of psychological wellness) is to choose to operate within a secure structure. This gives power to the organization and security to the individual as well.

Young people are the future. If you care for the present, you have to care for the future. The measure of your love of life is the measure of your concern for young people.

- Eric Perlman

Organizationally we have choices. In building the culture of our schools we need to decide between

solid solutions	or	**quick fixes**
risk taking	or	**risk avoidance**
applied creativity	or	**mindless conformity**
smart work	or	**busy work**
decisiveness	or	**paralysis by analysis**
simplication	or	**needless complication**
quality work	or	**fast work**
loyalty	or	**turnover**
quiet effective behavior	or	**squeaking joints**
working together	or	**working against**

Remember the initial question raised in this chapter? **"Ask yourself why you are doing what you are doing?"** Addressing choices can help you determine where you are, which, like *Alice in Wonderland*, will help you determine where you'd like to go.

Incentives are powerful motivators. Virtually all of learning comes down to incentives. If we get the incentives right then people will be motivated to succeed. If I desire to learn something, the likelihood is strong that I shall. I want to learn what I value, or am convinced by people whom I value that what I am learning has some future significance. (Purkey's Learning Triangle - Chapter 1.)

With outward success, the motivation is reinforced and becomes internalized. I want to learn what interests me, what is fun, and what those special teachers and/or colleagues tell me is important. These truths are evident for 60 year olds as well as 12 year olds.

Yet within schools, as Ted Sizer in his superb work, *Horace's Compromise*, (1984) tells us...

> *The most common motivating devices are lures and threats, sugar lumps and sticks. The stick is firmly in place in American schools.*

Threat as a motivating device is as ineffective as it is superficially efficient. Hostility gets in the way of learning. Involvement and a sense of ownership assists learning.

Here's an illustration that demonstrates that even tart apples can be made into apple sauce.

In an eighth grade class the teacher, John DeBaun, needed to leave the class momentarily. In the teacher's absence, a 6 foot 3 inch student, who was on the four year plan in our three year school, went to the window and "digitally acclaimed" the physical education class that was passing below on their way to the athletic field.

Picture this – huge boy – arm, hand and finger outstretched, classmates giggling – teacher returns to the class and catches the action in full bloom. Instant silence. All eyes turn to the teacher awaiting a response.

We pause to let you think of how you would react were you the teacher... We continue.

The teacher didn't say a word and instead gestured to the student to leave the window and sit in the seat at the front of the room. "LATER..." said the teacher, just loud enough for all to hear. "Later" comes when the rest of class has been dismissed and the student is addressed by the teacher in this way.

"I see you are impressed with hand gestures, yet your choice of them in school is not good. This is what you will do to learn more acceptable ones than you used today. I've spoken to the librarian and she has set aside a book on sign language for your use. By tomorrow afternoon you will be able to give me an original sentence or two in sign language. One possibility might be, 'I'm sorry for disturbing class yesterday. I promise not to do it again.' I'm sure you will develop a good one. If you can't come up with an alternative, do the one I just mentioned. You will also look through the book to see if the gesture you used is in there. If it is not, we'll spend an hour after school tomorrow discussing correct communication in school."

Well done. The teacher deferred action by his initial response, "Later..." which enabled everyone to know that the situation would be dealt with, and that the teacher was in charge. "Later..." gave the teacher an opportunity to think through his response, and to contact the librarian. Assessment, analysis, action – the teacher did a beautiful job in answering **what he was doing and why**! He looked to the circumstances and made a teachable moment out of adversity. And, he made the punishment fit the crime.

Now it's your turn. A number of scenarios that actually occur in schools follow. Think them through yourself or get a group of colleagues together and brainstorm responses. Perhaps you can use these examples as a "prelim" to an actual analysis of your school's current practices.

SCHOOL ANALYSIS EXERCISE

I. PRACTICE. The P.A. and bell system are used throughout the day to summon the custodian and/or principal to the office. The system is used frequently.

   What does this say to others?
   Alternative(s)?
            ....

II. POLICY. Report card grades for English, Math, Science and Social Studies are on a "letter basis" (A through F). All other courses (Art, Foreign Language, Health, Physical Education, etc.) are Pass/Fail. Further, only the "big four" count toward Honor Roll computation and promotion considerations.

   What does this say to others?
   Alternative(s)?
            ....

III. PROCEDURE. Afternoon announcements begin from 5 to 8 minutes prior to dismissal during the last period of the day. Morning announcements are repeated during this time. There is often 3 or 4 minutes down time in between the conclusion of the announcements and dismissal.

What does this say to others?
Alternative(s)?

....

IV. PRACTICE. A team of teachers arrive at different times   (9:52 - 9:58) to a scheduled 9:50 meeting with a student's parents. Three of the four teachers bring and are drinking coffee. The counselor who called the meeting (at the request of the teachers) begins the meeting at 10:00.

What does this say to others?
Alternative(s)?

....

V. POLICY. Seventh and eighth grade students who participate in either Band or Chorus do not take the ten week General Music course and student athletes are exempted from physical education class.

What does this say to others?
Alternative(s)?

....

VI. PROCEDURE. Students who have received disciplinary referrals and are to be seen by the Assistant Principal have their names broadcast over the P.A. system a minute prior to the bell for the dismissal of the period.

What does this say to others?
Alternative(s)?

....

The previous exercises can provide effective means of identifying implicit objectives and analyzing practices. ***analysis*** is a process inherent in effective organizations, and when coupled with the type of ***assessment*** you just experienced leads to positive ***action***.

A powerful story that underscores this point is brilliantly told by Joel Arthur Barker in his videotape, *Discovering the Future (The Business of Paradigms, (1988)*. It pertains to the watch-making business.

Barker begins this segment of his tape by asking what nation in 1968 dominated the watch-making business and had done so for over a hundred years? He answers.

Switzerland, of course. In this year the Swiss controlled 80% of all the profits with over 65% of the market share. Talk about market domination! Yet 10 years later their prime position had slipped to less than 10% of the market! In the ensuing three years they released over 50,000 of their 65,000 watch workers.

Today which nation virtually dominates the watch-making industry? Yes, Japan. Yet looking back to 1968 they had only a minor role. What happened to a nation that had been known for watch-making excellence and product innovation?

The answer may be found on your wrist right now. The battery powered, thousand times more efficient, totally electronic, quartz movement watch. This new concept soon replaced the old spring-wound model and almost totally captured the market.

It was a brilliant idea. Would you like to know who invented this marvelous watch? The answer may be a surprise to you; for it was the Swiss themselves! Yet when the researchers presented their invention to their home offices they were rejected out of hand. After all, the new watches didn't have a main spring; didn't have bearings; got its power from a battery. It had no chance to replace the product that for years had been so successful.

The Swiss manufacturers were so convinced of the correctness of their argument that they didn't patent what their researchers had developed. Later that year at the Annual Watch Congress when the watch was displayed, Texas Instruments and Seiko walked by, took one look and the rest is history.

The Swiss had been blinded by their successes and habits and couldn't see another approach to making their product. When faced with a new concept they rejected it simply because it didn't fit the patterns and rules they were already so good at."

While this story is about business and world markets it has significance for all of us in education. Past success guarantees us little, if the rules change. Past performance may be an indication of our talents, but it limits our potential if we refuse to grow and change. Assessment and analysis are fine in providing data to consider. Yet, *action* is necessary if we are to avoid the tragic outcomes of the Swiss watch makers' story. Be careful, for as Barker suggests,

Your successful past may block your vision to the future.

Periodically calling time out and figuring out why you are doing what you are doing, and asking also what you should be doing, will keep your empowered school on the cutting edge of growth. An openness to new ideas enables you to keep wide the doors to the future without denying the effectiveness of the past.

When teachers, staff, and administration all have the same goals, when all analyze critically their actions, explicitly select strategies to achieve them, and welcome new ideas in the process, positive sparks are ignited and things happen. When they don't, very little happens, and organizational decay is likely to set in.

How people may effectively and harmoniously work together in understanding the elements of empowerment are in store for us in Chapter 6. 🍎

Chapter 6

Empowerment: Unleashing Personal, Professional and Organizational Potential

After dying, a man found himself at the gates of hell. He was sobered by the fact that he needed to spend some time here in order to reflect on the life he had led. He envisioned what hell would be as he waited to enter. As time passed, the gates swung open.

He was surprised to enter a well-lit room overlooking a gorgeous vista replete with spring flowers and the light green colors of new growth. It was beautiful – not at all what he had expected. In the center of the room was a large table with an extravagant amount of food. His senses were filled with the sounds of song birds from outside, the smells of a wonderful meal and the bright, cheery colors of spring.

At that moment, a large dinner bell sounded, and he with others filled the seats surrounding the food-laden table. He was startled to see how physically and spiritually emaciated the people were. Waiters paused until all were seated and then left and returned with knives, forks and spoons, all of which were at least six feet in length and very heavy. The people were starving because they could not feed themselves with their utensils.

He was relieved when his stay was over and it was time to go to heaven. He was hungry. With great anticipation, he arrived at the gates and upon entering was shocked to see a close duplicate of the first scene in hell. There was a full table, wonderful view, the smell of good food and the sounds of new life. He was further startled when the same sound announced the mealtime. However, there was a noticeable difference. The people that filled the chairs around him were well fed, rosy-cheeked and radiant. He thought he knew the difference between heaven and hell. In heaven there had to be eating utensils that allowed you to feed yourself.

You can imagine his shock when the waiters brought in the same huge utensils that he had come to dread in hell. After the utensils were laid out, he discovered the true difference between heaven and hell. The people in heaven fed the people across from them.

This old story adapted from a retelling by Bill Elberty of Rochester, New York is apropos.

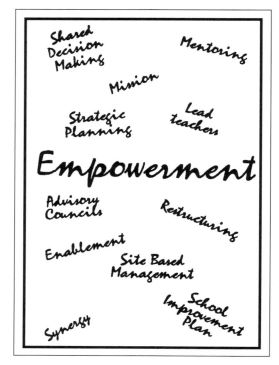

Many terms are being used to describe school organization issues.

In an empowered school people both value and assist one another. Whether falling in the category of teamwork, personal motivation or synergy, people who choose to make a difference make positive connections in the work place. Robert Frost once said:

The best place to be is where you are, if you have the wit to make it so!

If we do indeed have "the wit to make it so" then we can create an empowered school for the belief that *we can* make a difference is a key element in positively influencing organizational growth.

If our attempts reside in a well founded philosophy (chapter 1); we truly understand our clientele (chapter 2); come to grips with ourselves and are willing to face new paradigms of thinking (chapter 3 and 4); and assess, analyze and are willing to take action (chapter 5); then the poet, Frost, no doubt would be predisposed to agree that we were well on our way to a successful journey.

This chapter covers that journey. It deals with the elements of empowerment, the culture of an effective organization, personal touchstones and examples, and practical suggestions for your use. This chapter will link previous discussions as did the understanding of those good souls who recognized that feeding the people across from them enabled all to reach a heavenly state.

The powerful need all of us have to make what we do meaningful is possible when we connect the new with the "previously understood." I encourage you to engage in the creative process of blending the elements of your success and knowledge with the information of this chapter. Doing so may help you to reaffirm the direction of your existing quest, and/or to engage in a remarkable new adventure in which you can take a significant part.

So many terms – concepts
That seem brand new. I know
They aren't needed by me, but
They surely are needed by you...

There is a ring of truth to this vignette. The "other guy" does need to be in touch with the previously identified terms and the concepts behind them; but if we are to contribute to the empowerment of our organizations, so do we.

Twenty years ago in wandering through the hallowed halls of Teachers College, Columbia, I spied on a professor's door what has become a "classic" regarding passing the buck.

PASSING THE BUCK

The College Professor
Such rawness in a student is a shame; but high school preparation is to blame.

The High School Teacher
Good Heavens, what crudity, the boy's sure a fool; the fault, of course, is in the junior high school.

The Junior High School Teacher
From such youth I should be spared; they sent them up so unprepared.

The Elementary School Teacher
A cover for the dunce's stool; why was he ever sent to school?

The Kindergarten Teacher
Never such a lack of training did I see. What kind of person must the mother be?

The Mother
Poor child, but he is not to blame. His father's folks were all the same.

Author unknown

If we take an objective look at how educators traditionally think, the aforementioned poetic logic is not difficult to understand. In schools we tend to look to others at the grade or level below ours to blame – serve as scapegoats – for the inferior student material we have to teach. We elevate our efforts and denigrate the good works of others in far too many ways.

Even in the same district, it is rare to identify adequately our connectedness – our functioning as synchronous pieces of the same jigsaw puzzle. Though we may claim curricular awareness, we do not really pursue the integration of our instruction to earlier or subsequent instructional levels. The practice is inexcusable, but common.

In the preceeding poem, with the exception of his "father's folks," everyone gets a chance to blame someone else. Yet as the aforementioned current "buzz words" (advisory, mentoring, strategic planning, etc.) imply, we are called upon now, perhaps more than ever before, to be **interdependent.** After years of placing blame we now receive a clarion call to action.

However, **independence** is a strong value in our society. After all aren't we training the young to be just that? Don't we value being able to stand on one's own feet, to possess true grit, to be rock solid, able to cope, and able to survive?

Perhaps we do talk out of both sides of our mouth on this issue. We speak of organizational connectedness, yet cling to strong autonomous foundations. The result looks like a modern day Trojan horse. Our schools often move with a painfully slow locomotion if they move at all. The administrator sits atop the beast – much like the elephant's mahout – beating it with sticks and chains to spur it to action. Eventually the thing moves one one-hundredth of a degree to the right or the left – and the mahout (principal) praises the beast, effusively bleating or extolling the virtues of this movement. I'm not so sure that this monolithic beast is moving forward as much as the background upon which it is painted is moving backward.

Notwithstanding the integrity of our individual uniqueness, not withstanding our own individual autonomy, we truly are dependent on one another in our organizations. If we are to spur the behemouth to significant action, pulling together, **interdependence**, is the key.

The call to action in any empowered human enterprise is powerfully captured by the highly inspirational piece, *THE COLD WITHIN*. (It would be well to read this poem again so it's meaning can fully sink in.)

THE COLD WITHIN

Six humans trapped by happenstance
In black and bitter cold;
Each one possessed a stick of wood,
Or so the story's told.

Their dying fire in need of logs,
The first woman held hers back,
For on the faces around the fire
She noticed one was black.

The next man looking cross the way
Saw one not of his church,
and couldn't bring himself to give
The fire his stick of birch.

The third one sat in tattered clothes,
He gave his coat a hitch.
Why should his log be put to use
To warm the idle rich?

The rich man just sat back and thought
Of the wealth he had in store,
And how to keep what he had earned
From the lazy, shiftless poor.

The black man's face bespoke revenge
As the fire passed from his sight.
For all he saw in his stick of wood
Was a chance to spite the white.

And the last of this forlorn group
Did naught except for gain.
Giving only to those who gave
Was how he played the game.

The logs held tight in death's still hands
Was proof of human sin.
They didn't die from the cold without;
They died from the cold within.

Anonymous

Passing the buck had a bittersweet humor to it. *The Cold Within* hits hard at the latent prejudice inherent in each of us. Both attack our biases. Empowered organizations enable people to come to grips and draw out the inherent strength within. We must not seek to lay blame. We cannot operate as independent entities, islands unto ourselves. And perhaps more importantly, we must know how to let go of past hurt and prejudice in order to deal with our present and future potential. This latter point deals with a concept that might be labelled *forgiveness*.

Forgiveness

is not	*is*
- I absolve you	- Letting go
- Condoning your previous actions	- Moving on and beyond
- Punishing forever	- Peace
- Forgetting	- Growing
- Hoping they suffer	- Doing for yourself
- Pulling back	- Contributing

This comparison, adapted from Sid Simon, frames the open, healthful attitude necessary for organizational development and movement beyond the real and/or imaginary problems of the past.

A few years ago at a scheduled conference day all staff came together to deal with the effective schools research. After the obligatory keynote speech, the staff clustered into small groups to work on specific tasks. One group had as its task the development of a proper definition for the term **synergy**. After stumbling for twenty minutes with some rather obtuse thoughts, a talented group member who just happened to be a night custodian, came up with this definition.

Synergy is when
$$1 + 1 = 3$$

Beautiful for its simplicity, its eloquence, its power!

In an empowered synergistic organization, the whole is greater than the sum of its parts. In such an organization, everyone can and does make a difference; and the talents of people go well beyond the roles they usually play. People may seemingly have a single dimension job but their talents are multi-dimensional.

Six people trapped by happenstance in black and bitter cold, did not employ the power within and succumbed. We need to draw not only from the *obvious energy* in the organization but to establish a structure that taps the *latent talent* inherent within. Consider this analogy.

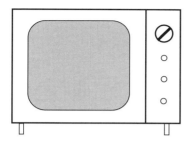

Television sets of today have advanced circuitry and as such they produce a picture the instant you turn them on. Yet few of us realize that even when the set is off, it is drawing a small amount of current from the wall socket, enough to keep it in a constant state of readiness.

The latent talent of an organization is very much like a charge of energy – when challenged, it responds. And if that talent pool is regarded as an integral part of a dynamic enterprise, it becomes an indispensable component in the organizational scheme of "the way we do things around here." Pigeon-holing, closing out connectedness, essentially creates an artificial pecking order and limits people's contributions to the organization. When 1 + 1 = 3 then the sticks of everyone feed the fires that illuminate and warm all of us.

Remember the popular puzzle in which you are asked to connect nine dots with *four straight lines without lifting your pencil* from the paper? Try it.

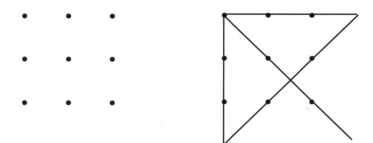

In order to solve the puzzle, most need to change their pattern of thinking. The dots imply a closed plane, but in order to solve the puzzle, you need to go beyond your limited patterns of previous thinking and open up to new possibilities. There is no way to solve the puzzle unless you expand your range of possibilities (go beyond the implied limits of the dots). We must be open to differing ways of thinking in order to solve organizational puzzles as well. A narrow perspective about how school is supposed to operate limits our creativity. When thinking is narrow, when we see just one way to deal with a problem, our potential is reduced.

As we discovered in Chapter 5 questioning beliefs opens up new patterns and possibilities. But we need to have some rock solid beliefs upon which to build the empowered school. One belief is that everyone can make a positive difference in the life of a child. Graphically this is what it might look like:

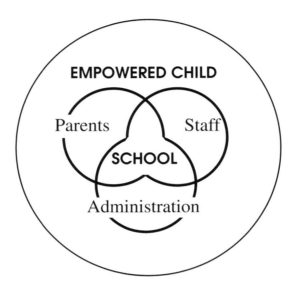

The positive influence of parents, staff, and administration is the central core in empowering children.

The empowered school establishes this common interdependence and mutuality of purpose. However, this is easier said than done. The parents who acknowledge that school personnel have an intensive period of time to influence positively their children, the staff who realize that parents send their very best to school and desire the best for those children; and administrators who know that they are the catalysts or glue that binds the elements together, all stand a very good chance of contributing to that empowered school.

Some pointed and probing questions that these three groups might consider are set forth in the following figure.

HOW INVOLVED AM I?

for PARENTS	for STAFF	for ADMINISTRATION
What interest do I take in school, and how do I show this to my kids?	Will the teaching actions I take be shared with parents? How?	What interest do I take in school, and how do I show this to my kids?
How do I really view the school's role? If it is negative, where does this feeling come from, and how can I change it?	Do I fear parental pressure? If so, where does this feeling come from, and how can I change it?	How do I really view the school's role? If it is negative, where does this feeling come from, and how can I change it?
Do I have stereotypes about school personnel that get in the way of positive feelings about the school?	Do my stereotypes about parents and administrators prevent successful communications?	Do I have stereotypes about school personnel that get in the way of positive feelings about the school?
Do I write notes or letters to school personnel or tell them personally that I appreciate what they are doing for my children?	Do I make it common practice to communicate positive things to parents about their children?	Do I write notes or letters to school personnel or tell them personally that I appreciate what they are doing for my children?
Do I take the time to care and let my kids know it?	Do I take the time to care and let my kids know it?	Do I take the time to care and let my kids know it?

Other questions could readily be added. These examples are designed to help people walk conceptually in the proverbial moccasins of others. The commonality for all three components is to reach and positively teach our children. The school that is empowered looks like this:

$$\frac{\text{Teachers (Staff)}}{\text{Enriched}} + \frac{\text{Parents}}{\text{Enlightened}} + \frac{\text{Leaders}}{\text{Enthusiastic}} + \frac{\text{Students}}{\text{Esteemed}} = \frac{\text{School}}{\text{Empowered}}$$

**The Common Denominator is
Empowerment**

TEACHERS who know their craft well, understand their roles as interdependent professionals, reach out to establish trusting relationships, and press their limits for personal and professional growth are ***enriched*** and actively create an empowered school.

Parents who model their belief in education to their children, support effective instruction, seek understanding and personal growth by learning new things, provide quality interactions with people who postively influence their children are ***enlightened*** and may be counted on to contribute to an empowered school.

Leaders who understand that what they *are* is far more important than what they *say*, establish opportunities for open communications for staff and parents, recognize that their role as middle managers *does not mean* that they have to take *middle ground positions* on issues, demonstrate leadership in positively influencing others, possess the fire, joy and conviction that what they do is tremendously important are ***enthusiastic*** and serve in a visionary role in helping others to reach an uncommon success.

The student-teacher relationship is all-important.

Students who know they attend a school that cares about them, have adults in their lives who value them and encourage their success, understand that limits exist so that they can make decisions within secure boundaries, feel unconditionally regarded as valuable human beings, exude self-confidence and who are secure are ***esteemed*** and achieve success.

Each school that reaches out to its community, celebrates its successes, and has a clear/unified purpose, has the potential to become an empowered school. Whenever dominant organizational thinking limits opportunities for positive involvement and ownership, the dysfunctional elements of an organization tend to increase. Wearing blinders to opportunity by stereotyping parents as not caring, viewing a teacher's calendar as part-time work, or typecasting administrators as "Caspar Milquetoasts," denigrates individuals and denies organizational health. Clear choices exist that distinguish the dysfunctional organization from the healthy organization.

THE DYSFUNCTIONAL ORGANIZATION	THE HEALTHY ORGANIZATION
Characterized by WIN/LOSE interpersonal and intergroup relationships	Characterized by COLLABORATIVE WIN/WIN interpersonal and intergroup relationships
Leadership is RESTRICTIVE, CORRECTIVE, AUTHORITARIAN, and FORMAL	Leadership is SHARED, CONSENSUAL, and INFORMAL
TRIVIAL PROBLEMS are seen as important issues	Energies are directed toward SUBSTANTIVE ISSUES
GOSSIP is rampant	Communications are OPEN, POSITIVE, and SUPPORTIVE
Defensiveness is common and RESISTANCE to CHANGE is high	People ASSESS, ANALYZE, and ACT in order to progress and grow
Little identification with common goals – ISOLATION is high	Organizational goals are known and accepted – INTERDEPENDENCE is high
People are frustrated, unhappy, anxious, insecure, apathetic and lack interest in their work	People are authentic, enthusiatic, open, energetic, productive, happy and secure

A clear alternative – *dysfunction* or *health*! Who wouldn't choose the latter, especially if one assesses the impact the former has on the personal, psychological and professional worth of each of us. Yet we have to choose, not so much by our words but by our actions.

THE CULTURE OF AN EMPOWERED SCHOOL

Several years ago I extensively studied the research on school culture. (Loosely defined, culture is what we do in an organization; climate is how we feel about it.) Matt King and Jon Saphier (1985) conducted summative studies in this area. They developed a "school culture tree" depicting the elements inherent in an effective culture. Taking a leaf so to speak from their work, I developed an Apple Tree of an Empowered Organization.

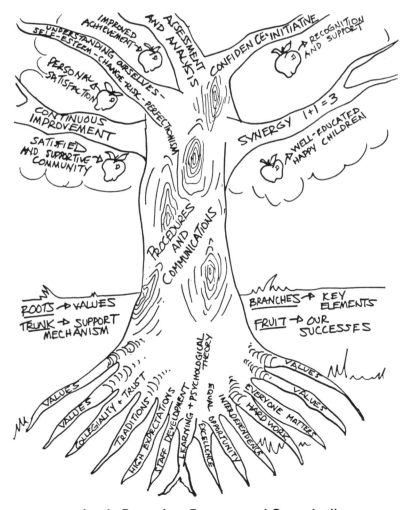

Apple Tree of an Empowered Organization

The roots keep our tree secure against strong winds and the elements of challenge. Anchored deep below the surface, our roots are values. Values are the emotional rules by which a culture governs itself. They represent the accumulated wisdom by which the organization structures and disciplines itself. Values are the reminders that individuals obey to bring order and meaning into their personal lives. Organizations, of course, could have been included in that statement.

Values education often has the more conservative elements of a community shrieking about the school assuming a parental responsibility. But the values referred to are simply those basic all-but-universal ones such as:

- collegiality and trust
- traditions of success
- high expectations for all
- life-long learning
- excellence
- equal opportunity
- hard work and values that reinforce
- the worth of each and every individual and the taproot, the deepest divining root that holds our tree fast is how we regard the
- theoretical foundations of learning, psychology, and human development

But today when the journalistic wags sensationalize the decay of our society and educational system, what of values education and the school's role in guiding our children? The school is the legal agency established by society and supported by public taxes to educate youth. Its job is to imbue the child with societal norms, basic knowlege, fundamental skills, and the human values required for a successful adult life. Its task is formidable, its challenge great, and its resources limited.

As Walt Kelly's cartoon character, POGO stated:

We have met the enemy – and he is us.

There is no choice but to teach values to our children. Were we not to do so, we would indeed become an enemy to the best interests of our students, our community, and our culture. The empowered school provides solid values' education and a deep concern for the ethical mores of our society. Great educators have always emphasized the importance of values in working with highly impressionable students.

The trunk of the tree is the substantive structure. Here we find our *procedures* and *communications*. Organizational maintenance, efficiency and operations depend on this structure. People who are secure are not disempowered or dysfunctional. People who depend on an efficient, well-run organization, need not deal with chaos or indecision. Those people are able to "branch out," and branching out enables us to extend ourselves beyond minimal boundaries. While the fundamental values we all share securely root us, the effectiveness of our communications and procedures provide a base for the branching process of our growth and development.

The main branches of our tree are: **synergy, confidence and initiative, assessment, analysis, understanding ourselves, self-esteem, change, risk, perfectionism and continuous improvement.**

Our notion of synergy is that everyone counts. Confident that we can make a difference, we do. In an interdependent organization, one plus one truly equals three.

Confident initiative means that people who are in touch with themselves know that though teaching for twenty years, they can keep the essence of previous successes and still try new things. In that way the twenty year teacher does not do the same year twenty times. That attitude keeps one alive and growing.

Assessment and analysis enables us to keep in touch and to embrace new alternatives and ways of interpreting organizational issues and effectiveness (Chapter 5).

Understanding change, risk, perfectionism, is basically a matter of understanding ourselves vis-a-vis our organization. Knowing our motivators and placing them in perspective helps us achieve a higher sense of organizational connectedness.

Continuous improvement is the essence of all effective organizations. Success is not a destination but a *process* of healthful growth and development. Being in touch with the knowledge base, enlarging one's abilities by attending professional seminars, reading to sharpen your insights enables the *quality of your journey* to be first class.

The culture "tree" of an empowered school has as its life-force *growth.* Though at times subtle and at other times rapid, *action* **is the growth element of an organization.** The desire to consciously move forward lies at the center.

Further applying the apple tree analogy, organizations experience various seasons or phases. The latency of an organization is like *winter* – somber, quiet, possessing potential but not actively demonstrating its capabilities.

Spring for our organizational tree is a time of rebirth. Wonderful buds of new thinking flower and are resplendent. Yet their time is transitory, for as many ideas are prone to have moments in the sun, only when they are "pollinated" or strengthened by the thoughts of others do they germinate and become fruit.

And in the *summer* of an organization's development, proper care and nourishment enable ideas to grow and ripen. As the degree of support influences their size and grandeur, the apples become recognizable and have an undeniable uniqueness. Though similar in appearance, each has a shape and character of its own.

When **fall** comes to our organizational tree we are ready to savor the fruits of our efforts. The fruits of our school tree are numerous including:

- community recognition and support
- staff who are alive with the fervor
  of their acomplishments
- satisfied and supportive parents
- appreciation and recognition for our efforts
- a deep personal sense of satisfaction

The empowered school has seasons in its development. Simply declaring a school "empowered" certainly does not make it so. As in the well-rooted system of values of our tree, we have to demonstrate hard work, a clarity of purpose and **patience.**

The following story illustrates adolescence, self-esteem, and the talent inherent in all organizations. If you enjoy kinesthetic learning, and/or you would like a fruit snack, get an apple, a knife and a napkin, though there is no need to have these items to enjoy the story. However, your enjoyment may be enhanced by following the directions after you read the story.)

The Little Apple Tree

A little apple tree lived in the heart of a huge forgotten forest. Being little, he was blocked from the sky by the branches of majestic pine trees. At night he would hear them talking about how beautiful were the stars. One day the little apple tree cried out to the Great Spirit. "Oh Great Spirit when will I too be able to see the stars?" The Great Spirit said,"In time, in time, little tree – try your very hardest and one day you too will see the stars." Soon the little apple tree noticed changes in himself, beautiful pink flowers adorned his branches.

Again the apple tree cried out – "Oh Great Spirit, when oh when will I see the stars?" "In time, in time," replied the voice, "be patient and one day you too will see the stars."

And the little apple tree was patient and the flowers fell and were replaced by hard little spheres. The little apple tree continued to try his hardest and was patient as the summer had come and gone, and on a clear crisp fall night,the little apple tree raised his voice to the Great Spirit. "Oh Great Spirit, when oh when will I see the stars?"

And the Great Spirit said, "Little apple tree you have indeed tried your hardest...and indeed you have been patient, now is the time for you to see the stars."

And because you also have been patient and because you deserve it, it now is time for you to see the stars as well.

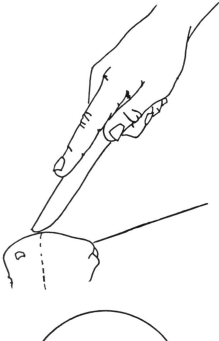

Take the apple and put it on a flat cutting surface. Whoa – don't cut it the way you usually do. Chances are you've placed it just as it hung on the tree – stem up. Lay it on its side stem to your left hand side, apple bottom to your right hand side (west/east) Now with your knife make a north/south cut through the center cutting the apple into two equal halves. Now you can see the stars.

Time, nurturance, patience, and then slicing things a bit differently can reveal the star quality in an organization and indeed in all of us. Considering a variety of ways to effectively function within an oganization can produce unexpected gifts. The seasons of organizational empowerment are linked and advance each previous stage. Like the apple tree of the empowered organization, there is star quality inherent in each person and each school – if only we know how to tap it.

Remember the page of terms toward the front of the chapter? *Shared decision-making, mission, strategic planning* and *restructuring* were just a few. As a building principal I heard a number of these terms and was skeptical. Weren't these new terms just flashes in the pan? Were they something sinister lurking on the horizon, or worse yet were they really appropriate and could they force me to change?

*We must never forget that the light at the
end of the tunnel might just be that of
an oncoming train.*

So faced with uncertainty, I began to assess myself and to reach out to the knowledge base and become enmeshed in study to learn more about the "light at the end of the tunnel." These findings may prove helpful for you as they have helped to empower my thinking and professional capabilities.

Five Perspectives on Empowerment

VIEW #1

- Empowerment **is** sharing a vision and purpose with others.

- Empowerment **is not** relinquishing one's responsibility.

A person who aims at nothing has a target he can't miss. Genius is seeing a target no one else sees and hitting it dead center. There are times when the principal sees things that others don't and initiates a process that enables the team to hit the bull's eye. There are many times that groups have shared their vision with the principal. Leaders who constantly *defer* rather than *contribute* to the group relinquish their responsibility. Leaders do not wait for things to happen around them. Collaboratively sharing a vision empowers all. Being open and receptive to all points of view magnifies success.

VIEW #2

- Empowerment **is** a time-tested principle of healthy organizations.

- Empowerment **is not** a revolutionary concept.

History is replete with examples of empowerment. Consider the work of W. Edwards Deming. In the late 1920's Deming approached the captains of American industry with research evidence to support his claim of a way to increase worker productivity, upgrade quality, and provide substantive organizational improvement. American industry turned its back on this scholar.

One person who didn't was General Douglas MacArthur, a man who was to play a significant role in and after World War II. MacArthur surveyed the devastation of Japan particularly noting the havoc that the military-industrial complex had caused. The economy was in shambles. MacArthur assessed the situation and brought in Deming. The rest is history.

Deming's teachings brought sweeping change to Japan's industrial capacity and economy. A world leader today, Japan has served as a model for American companies by its success in productivity, product quality, and worker empowerment. American industry made many pilgrimages to Japan to analyze Japanese successes with "Theory Z" management techniques and the like. American industry and schools would have been well advised to have listened closely to Deming's messages presented over 60 years ago! His ideas took root in war torn Japan because their industrialists committed themselves to a course of action congruent with Deming's beliefs. Initial successes made believers out of even the most skeptical.

In the early 90's, Deming is talking to superintendents about the need to reframe districts through systematic, organized change. Will we repeat the errors of the captains of industry by once more holding on to what *is* rather than creating what *should be*? An ostrich can supposedly bury its head in the sand. And although people supposedly cannot, business did so years ago. Will schools do so?

VIEW #3

- Empowerment **is** a participatory developmental process with opportunities for all.

- Empowerment **is not** a "top down" notion.

The term *autoritas*, from the Latin, loosely translates to be "support from below to assist the organizational mass above". The concept is that those who lead best do so when they support others. The ***trunk*** of our culture tree deals with procedures and communications and similarly the second level of our communications mountain, ***maintenance***, deals with procedural support. Both anchor higher level activity and communications. In similar fashion, in an empowered organization management (the traditional *top*) supports what has traditionally been the *bottom*. It's like an inverted pyramid. The experience of Ford Motor Company provides a clarifying example.

Ford has undergone a significant restructuring in the last decade. The work being done today in Ford plants would confound yesterday's workers who had experienced differing work configurations, social arrangements, and management systems. The opportunity for workers to be accountable as a group for their production area, to have an expanded interdependence and impact on the development of the total product and to function in decentralized, quality circle groups was unheard of previously. Employee involvement in decision-making which makes it possible for any line worker to shut down the assembly line to correct a flaw, was unknown a decade ago. Heretofore, only management could make such a decision.

In school, management supports and "props up" the organization. As the administration's singlular authority is replaced by teacher and parent committees who make decisions previously centrally made, the good manager is one who helps establish a system, influences by example, and encourages the work of subordinates. The manager, through crisp and unambiguous assignments, develops standards of performance to which everyone ascribes.

Industry wants people who can collaborate effectively. In school we call that *cheating*. We need to change that attitude and pursue excellence by increasing our collaborative focus.

Remember, *excellence* can be attained if you:

- care more than others think is wise.
- risk more than others think is safe.
- dream more than others think is practical.
- expect more than others think is possible.

– Anonymous

Excellence comes to an organization when people are secure and exploit opportunities for involvement. Excellence comes to an organization when people press their limits for personal growth and are encouraged to do so. Organizational vision is enhanced when people have a stake in the operation. Schools are beginning to broaden that focus and close the isolationism that has existed for centuries.

VIEW #4

- Empowerment **is** strengthening all.

- Empowerment **is not** merely a proclamation nor is it disempowering some to empower others.

A highly publicized experiment in empowerment is occurring in a large city school district in New York. Amid blaring trumpets, the dawning of a new day in school empowerment was heralded. An outstanding teachers' contract was in place, advisory governing councils were established, and community linkage was expanded. Federal and corporate funds poured in to assist with the implementation design, a research center was located, and great things were projected.

The intention of this restructing plan was, and still is, quite positive. But during the second year when all publicized signals were that the empowerment process was a plan to establish collaborative structures and develop effective human relationships, the president of the teacher's association was quoted in the press as referring to members of the administrative unit as *The Blob*. His critical jibes were designed to undermine rather than build; to posture rather than to coalesce.

History will determine the effectiveness of this experiment in empowerment. Breaking people away from patterns via the infusion of large sums of money and declaring that empowerment is now in existence doesn't make it so. Developmental movement toward the vision of the organization based on harmony, mutuality of purpose and positive leadership does bring it about. Even though problems may exist, "tearing asunder" or disempowering some to empower others is dysfunctional. It may be argued that four years later this district is still dealing with the image of the change, with apparently little substantive progress. *Strengthening all* while the process of reframing occured would have helped immeasurably.

VIEW #5

- Empowerment **is** creating.

- Empowerment **is not** already created.

Effective empowerment is a process to help people enhance their capabilities and organizational successes. Though the word in the literal sense is a NOUN, in concept, it's a verb!

It would appear to be easy to wait for an empowerment experiment to work and then take that plan and transplant it into your operation. Nothing could be more ill advised. You need to become engaged in the *process of your own creation*. You need to develop critical elements for your plan and to use those as your guides.

Although we will learn much from those bold few who move to implement a heralded design, their plans are just that – *theirs!* And no one knows your organization better than you and your colleagues. You may bring in some outside consultant to help design your plan. But if the pieces are there, if the support network, personal focus, shared leadership, and desire to improve are present, you will have little need for external assistance.

This is also true with leadership. The need for a more autonomous or directive administrative presence changes when the momentum and confidence of the organization builds. The process of creating is incremental in its development as well.

THOUGHTS ON TEAM BUILDING

A central theme of this work is that in creating empowered schools we need to develop the talent inherent within the organization. Traditionally we have seldom done so.

Many organizational developers are ready to throw out the proverbial baby with the bath. *Renorming, reframing and restructuring* are some of the terms they utilize. The development of human potential calls for clarifying/expanding/ altering existing systems of rules, roles, and relationships so that schools may better serve today's purposes and develop more effective programs for the future. It is not necessary to redo the whole operation. We need to develop and showcase our talents first. The process needs developing confidence and collaboration. The process needs *teamwork!*

These two characters are in for a rude awakening when they try to float their craft. Teamwork essentially is heading in the same direction with effective communications to help you get there.

Unlike the mountain climbers, do we climb our organizational mountains with confidence, in the same direction, assisting one another along the way? Or like the canoe builders, are we in for a shock when we realize we have been working at cross purposes?

Reprinted with permission of Dan Roach

Recollect Albert Einstein's famous formula, $E = MC^2$. There is applicability to empowerment when his work is adapted like so:

$$If$$
$$Energy = MC^2$$
$$then$$

$$Empowerment = My\ Compentencies\ ^{Enriched}$$

Oliver Wendell Holmes said:

> **What lies behind and what lies ahead of us is of little importance when conpared to what lies within.**

If your point of view is positive, then it is likely that you will influence others positively. If what lies within is negative then the reverse is true. The application of your competencies enables you to empower others. In part that depends on your perspective.

Recall the old story of the two buckets in the well. Every time the one came up it would say, "This is truly a harsh and bitter job. For no matter how many times I come up full, I always go down empty." The other bucket replied through his laughter, "I'm different you see. For no matter how many times I go down empty, I always return full."

Though the members of teams often have differing perspectives, viewing the glass as half full rather than half empty certainly helps move the process of team building along the road to success. Creating, building, moving ahead – these are qualities inherent in a good team. Once again we face clear alternatives.

Wrecker

I watched them tearing a building down,
A gang of men in a busy town,
With a ho-heave-ho and a lusty yell,
They swung a beam and the side wall fell.

I asked the foreman, "Are these men skilled,
And the men you'd hire if you had to build?"
He gave a laugh and said, "No, indeed!
Just common labor is all I need.
I can easily wreck in a day or two
What builders have taken a year to do."

I thought to myself, as I went my way,
Which of these roles have I tried to play?
Am I a builder who works with care,
Measuring life by the rule and square?
Am I shaping my deeds to a well-made plan,
Patiently doing the best I can?

Or am I a wrecker, who walks the town,
Content with the labor of tearing down?

– H.S. Harp

In every organization a rainbow of talents, personalities, perspectives, and experiences exists. Some individuals may test our personal and professional patience, beyond the limit. Some may be so off-center that you'll wonder if they'll ever be a contributing member of your team. But the **acid test** of the empowered school is to explore and create ways to establish an environment where *all* can contribute. Whether it is the administrator, whose judgment is so suspect that you might think him capable of having sent a congratulatory magnum of champagne to the captain of the Exxon Valdez, or the sixth grade reading teacher who looks for any opportunity to sing the *Ride of the Valkyries* in German, in original costume, or the 8th grade department chairperson whose wardrobe moths retreat from, these and other such characters can test our resolve and present real challenges. We must ever be cognizant that our pre-judgements about people based on their uniqueness or idiosyncrasies can prevent their contributions from being presented or accepted. Be careful.

ORGANIZATIONAL LOYALTY

No matter what set of individuals you have in your organization, remember that, **the person who rows the boat seldom has time to rock it.** And when people become involved in charting the course of an organization, and see results for their efforts, another key element in organizational teamwork, **loyalty**, becomes a tangible outcome.

Psychologist Erik Erikson surmised that fidelity is a necessary stage in psychological growth. Explained Erikson (1968), "Fidelity is the ability to sustain loyalties freely pledged in spite of the inevitable contradictions and confusions of value systems." This ability is developed after the narcissism of adolescence has passed.

Loyalty comes with maturity. It requires a kind of unselfish giving up of some of one's personal autonomy. This sacrifice can only be made by a self-confident individual, one who feels no conflict or threat in giving loyalty to someone else or to an organization. When leaders or organizations turn their backs on their colleagues, apathy or organizational rejection occurs. When such institutions cannot earn the loyalty of their workers, team building cannot effectively occur. Compliant behavior may be achieved via the paycheck or fear of firing, but true loyalty and subsequent team building occurs when *trust that has been earned* exists. As in the investment company's commercial, we have to do so the old fashioned way – we need to earn it!

A synthesis of the data on self-esteem indicates that whether it be individuals, teams within the organization, or organizations themselves, the **building blocks of self-esteem** strongly pertain. Drawing from the research to apply it to thoughts on team building, I acknowledge the brilliance of Dennis Boike (1992), whose insights are woven throughout this tapestry. An easy way to remember the building blocks of self-esteem is to think of *SIAM* **with a C** added.

SECURITY...IDENTITY...AFFILIATION...MISSION and COMPE-TENCE. Each of these will be discussed and linked to the development of effective teams.

SECURITY is a strong sense of assuredness. The physiological needs (food, clothing, and shelter) of such individuals have been met. Their career is not in turmoil. Their comfort level is high and they know that there are others upon whom they can depend. The converse is true as well. If I can count on other people, then other people can count on me. I'm there for you and you're there for me. This gives the individual and the group an interconnected sense of powerfulness. Team security, like meal time in heaven, depends on people helping people.

TEAM ESTEEM

IDENTITY is knowing who you are, knowing from whence you've travelled and knowing that you possess the tools necessary to be what you want to be. Inherent in one's identity is the ability to have a realistic conception of roles, attributes, and physical characteristics. Knowing your skills and role and those of the other members of your team, helps to create empowered schools. Team identity requires synergy. (Remember 1 + 1 = 3.)

AFFILIATION is belonging to something outside of oneself. This is achieved first within the constellation of the family. Though the family usually remains a constant, later come social groups, scouts, class groups, sports teams, fraternal organizations, job related allegiances, church groups and the like. The human drive for connectedness is an underpinning for team participation – and team affiliation depends on mutually valued relationships.

MISSION is present when one has a clear direction and behavior is goal related. Directing one's energy at well-defined targets is a strength of an empowered or esteemed individual. In turn, when personal and professional goals, and individual and group goals, are in sync, positive sparks are ignited. Self-motivated individuals who set reasonable goals for themselves have power. This power impacts on the mission of the organization as well. Team mission depends on clearly articulated goals.

COMPETENCE comes from experiencing success in things one regards as important or valuable. Being aware of one's strengths enables one to accept one's weaknesses. Competent self-assured individuals compete *within themselves* for personal growth. These people acknowledge internally their accomplishments. They are self-validating and willingly acknowledge the accomplishments of others. Team competence depends on experiencing success and having individuals who possess strong standards of accomplishment.

The team builder is also an **ESTEEM** builder. Within the building block of **SECURITY** we build trusting relationships and create a positive and caring environment.

Within **IDENTITY** we build an awareness of our team's talents and unique qualities.

Within **AFFILIATION** we provide opportunities to discover the interests, capabilities and background of others. In so doing we encourage peer approval and support.

Within **MISSION** we enhance our team's abilities to make decisions, brainstorm alternatives, and project outcomes/consequences. Our behaviors facilitate goal direction and attainment.

Within **COMPETENCE** we pursue opportunities for success and target high and achievable expectations to press our limits and reach an uncommon success. Feedback to improve group weaknesses and to profit from mistakes becomes a part of group consciousness and data upon which corrrective actions may be based.

When teams and/or organizations develop high feelings of self-esteem and when these interactions become a matter of course, participation is not perfunctory. Organizational loyalty becomes a matter of team members "freely committing" in an atmosphere of mutual trust. In this arena abilities are respected and work is prized. Members of interdependent teams have much to offer one another. Those whose actions speak louder than their words help to establish empowered teams in empowered organizations.

Wilkerson's anatomy of an organization (1965) may be applied to team work. He says that in any group there are four basic types of bones:

Wishbones - Those who wish someone else would do the work.
Jawbones - Those who talk a greal deal but do little else.
Knucklebones - Those who "knock" what everyone else does.
Backbones - Those who get down and do the work.

Familiar? Know some people who fit one of the categories? Into which category do you fall?

A collection of competent individuals does not necessarily result in an effective team. Teamwork requires concessions, a willingness to subjugate an individual's desire to be a star to contribute to the star quality of the group. Understanding and utilizing group processes and pursuing task behaviors that accomplish team objectives are also needed.

On this latter point, team members often must be willing to give up well established roles, comfortable patterns, and preconceived judgments about others in order to effectively contribute. If we are to establish effective teams, we need to be willing to achieve **CONSENSUS** when reaching decisions.

Consensus means...
• all team members are willing to contribute
• all do contribute
• everyone's opinions are encouraged and heard
• everyone can paraphrase the issue
• everyone has an opportunity to express feelings about the issue
• those who disagree indicate a willingness to experiment for a certain period of time
• all members share or "own" the final decision
• all members agree to take responsibility for implementing the final decision

Consensus does not mean...
• a unanimous formal vote
• the result is everyone's first choice
• everyone agrees
• Questioning, conflict or resistance will be immediately overcome

(Arbuckle and Murray, 1989)

SMALL GROUP PROCESS

Reprinted with special permission of King Features Syndicate, Inc.

The stages of group development have been wryly identified as:

>*Forming*
>*Storming*
>*Norming*
>*Performing*

While groups don't really need to storm before they can perform, most groups do go through these stages. A different slant on stages is suggested from the general research developed in the business setting.

Stage I. **POLITENESS**. Relationships are superficial, simply polite. In this stage people tend to hold back their own feelings and ideas, and don't know the motives of the others. One or two members of the group tend to dominate.

Stage II. **CONFUSION and WHEEL SPINNING**. Now politeness and formality are replaced by chaos. Poor listening, arguing, members overlapping one another's conversations, leadership struggles, and poor planning predominate in this stage. Group performance is low although via luck and/or an individual member's contributions an acceptable level of achievement is gained. Member frustration and dissatisfaction with group performance, however, is common.

Stage III. **CONTROL and ORGANIZATION**. Members unhappy with the existing condition now seek redress on issues such as leadership, decision making, working together and controls. Detailed procedures are frequently formalized. Consensus begins to take shape although not yet completely. The prior experience of members carries the group in this stage. The group experience, though increasing in impact, is not a significant force as yet.

Stage IV. **LEARNING and PROBLEM SOLVING**. Here the group is beginning to mature. Members begin to express their real opinions concerning procedure and performance. Candor exists as members work toward common goals, trust is built, and procedures are modified as needed. The group experience "takes hold" and group decisions now replace prior organizational experience as a basis for decisions.

Stage V. **GROUP MATURITY**. The group is said to have gained maturity when it consistently solves problems creatively. An interesting dynamic of the mature group is when **the team** arrives at a correct decision despite the fact that one person in the group may have already had the totally correct solution. All members contribute, playing off the ideas and talents of one another. The group maintains a high level of productivity because all members cooperate rather than compete. Members both influence and are influenced by others. All contribute to group controls and keep focused on the task within agreed upon procedures.

Features of a Mature Group

- *Function as a unit.*
  - *Respect is readily given.*
    - *Members do not interrupt each other.*
- *Members fully participate.*
  - *On-task behavior predominates.*
    - *All contribute.*
- *Members are oriented toward a single goal.*
  - *Members share and work toward common purposes.*
    - *Members process and share information and skills.*
- *Members seek and receive suggestions, opinions and information.*
  - *They hear and consider all ideas.*
    - *Individual research lends to group knowledge.*

Not all groups reach maturity. Many have members who are unwilling or incapable of adapting in order to accommodate a greater allegiance. Group skills are not universally held and change is difficult for most. Regression also takes place periodically. This is natural. To keep a group's focus and effectivenss sharp requires constant effort. But keep in mind the alternative, humorously but poignantly presented in the following story.

You Can't Do It Alone

I am writing in response to your request concerning Block #11 on the insurance form which asks for "the cause of injuries" wherein I put "trying to do the job alone." You said you needed more information so I trust the following will be sufficient.

I am a bricklayer by trade and on the date of injuries I was working alone laying brick around the top of a four-story building when I realized that I had about 500 pounds of brick left over. Rather than carry the bricks down by hand, I decided to put them into a barrel and lower them by a pulley which was fastenened to the top of the building. I secured and flung the barrel out with the bricks in it. I then went down and untied the rope holding it securely to insure the slow descent of the barrel.

As you will note on Block #6 of the insurance form, I weigh 145 pounds. Due to my shock at being jerked off the ground so swiftly I lost my presence of mind and forgot to let go of the rope. Between the second and third floor, I met the barrel coming down. This accounts for the bruises and lacerations on my upper body. Regaining my presence of mind, again I held tightly to the rope and proceeded rapidly up the side of the building, not stopping until my right hand was jammed in the pulley. This acounts for my broken thumb.

Despite the pain, I retained my presence of mind and held tighly to the rope. At approximately the same time, however, the barrel of bricks hit the ground and the bottom fell out of the barrel. Devoid of the weight of the bricks, the barrel now weighed about fifty pounds. I again refer you to Block #6 and my weight.

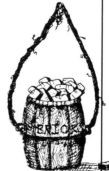

As you would guess, I began a rapid descent. In the vicinity of the second floor I met the barrel coming up. This explains the injuries to my legs and lower body. Slowed only slightly I continued my descent, landing on the pile of bricks. Fortunately my back was only sprained and the internal injuries were only minimal. I am sorry to report, however, that at this point I again lost my presence of mind and let go of the rope. As you can imagine, the empty barrel crashed down on me.

I trust this answers your concern. Please know that I am finished "trying to do the job alone."

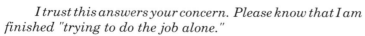

Author unknown

CONCLUSIONS

In this chapter we explored several notions of empowerment: the need to come together (to feed one another); the pointing fingers approach (where we passed the buck); interdependence (to avoid *The Cold Within*); synergy; a common de-nominator (empowerment); and healthy vs. dysfunctional organizations. We also climbed an apple tree and tasted the fruit; met up with five biases and found that the light at the end of the tunnel was illumination; dealt with what teams are and what techniques can be used to implement a team approach in an empowered school.

The impossibility of doing the job alone was made apparent. *Connectedness* magnifies individual's effectiveness and focuses the creative energies and potential within the organization. It is what empowered schools are all about.

All personnel of a school comprise its group. The touchstones and processes shared in this chapter can help the group become a team. While applying a clearly elicited plan through a unified team approach is highly advisable, conscious attention to the human factor increases the likelihood of success. Operating on the same wave length with clearly delineated tasks and specific timelines helps the task to be effectively and efficiently met.

In order to be effective the empowered school must:

- *know where it is heading,*

- *know why,*

- *have an idea of how to get there,*

    and

- *be willing to develop the attitudes, teamwork, and processes needed to achieve its objectives.*

With Frost's admonition spurring us to create the best place we can because we have the wit to make it so, we move to chapter 7 on **leadership**, certainly a key element in the empowered school. 🍎

Chapter 7
Leadership: The Essential Ingredient of Empowered Schools

In empowered schools teachers are leaders and principals are leaders of leaders.

In nearly every type of organization people have the capacity to assume leadership. The capacity is there, but whether individuals choose to lead or not is likely to depend on the encouragement that they receive from the officially designated leaders. Effective leadership develops leadership in others.

The recurring theme of this book is that **each and every person has worth** and the culture of the empowered school enables **all** to become leaders in some sense of the word. Leadership potential exists in cafeteria workers, teachers, secretaries, custodians, and all support personnel. And parents and students are not outside this "loop" of opportunity.

Increased ownership, increased enthusiasm, increased productivity, and increased influence with others (leadership) occurs when organizational connectedness increases. It is primarily a matter of **CAUSE** and **EFFECT**. A positive environment creates positive interdependence. Positive interdependence creates positive sharing. And positive sharing creates positive leadership. If we choose to empower schools, then we must create empowered leadership in those schools.

Changing notions of leadership have helped to improve the quality of our organizations today. It used to be easy to know who the leader was. The principal was *the* figurehead, the final authority. Today principals come in all shapes and sizes and in both genders. As viewed in the following diagram, leadership has undergone a dramatic metamorphosis from the time when "coach" was in the main office.

The Evolution of Authority

While we smile at the above, a strong argument can be mounted for further evolutionary steps around the board table as depicted on the next page.

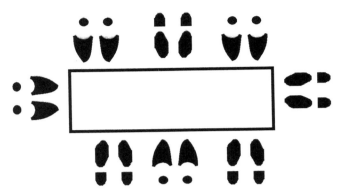

The latter diagram symbolizes the leader as "one among equals." Leaders may have clearly identified and differing roles that complement one another, but they are all leaders.

Lest we move too quickly, let's get back to the designated school leader...the principal. Don Johansen (1976) of the Minnesota Department of Education developed a list of variables that he claims will enable the uninitiated observer to identify the principal 98% of the time.

• The principal is the one whose desk look like a trash hauler's nightmare, but who walks around picking up scraps of paper in the halls.

• The principal is the one whose back has the funny kink in it and a blood pressure reading of 175/90, but does not hesitate to carry in extra chairs for a meeting or launch a basketball from halfcourt at the annual staff/ student contest.

• The principal is the one whose personal checkbook defies interpretation – but meticulously accounts for every penny of student activity funds.

• The principal is the one who holds three university degrees – yet spends a substantial percentage of time each day inspecting lavatories.

• The principal is the one whose nose is corroded from asbestos, locker rooms, chemistry experiments, paint and hair sprays – yet can pick out a tiny whiff of a controlled substance in a football crowd of 2,000.

• The principal is the one who schedules teachers, students, classes, rooms, special events, back to school nights, and the like in a complex maze – yet can't find the car in the supermarket parking lot.

• The principal is the one who relentlessly praises others for jobs well done – yet doesn't know how to accept praise when it is given in kind.

• Principals are the ones who read this checklist and smile because they do not take themselves seriously – yet who take the responsibility of the principalship most seriously.

Can you relate to this set of tongue-in-cheek criteria?

Despite the reality that people still look at the principal in a paternalistic/ maternalistic manner current research reveals that shared decision making is increasing the effectiveness of schools today.

People need to find a place where they're needed – where they fit.

This chapter will sample that trend and focus on how you can broaden the scope and effectiveness of leadership in your school or organization.

The phrase..."It's not the school, it's the principal of the thing" has a certain truth to it. But the old Welch book, *The Mabinogion*, rings the bell with clarity when it states:

"A Fo Ben Bid Bout" – He (she) who would lead must be a bridge!

In a school, everything important touches everything else of importance. Bridges are inevitable. As the stated leader in the organization the principal bridges to/and affects all others. The synergy of the empowered middle school plays off the strengths and contributions of all. Leadership bridges what *has been* and guides an on-going investigation of what *can* and *ought* to be.

If we presume that all decisions need to be made by or at least cleared through one person, organizational paralysis will occur. Similarly when a committee takes over the sole responsibility for what previously was an individual's responsibility, then organizational paralysis can occur as well.

Keep in mind, however, that a task taken on by a committee does not automatically mean that the outcome will be more efficient, more effective, or even more representational than when done by an individual. The old joke applies – *What is a camel? A horse that's been designed by a committee.* In our empowered organizations we need to have an effective blend of individual and group initiative so that the horse remains a horse and the organization can gallop like the wind. This balance is not difficult to achieve.

Yet in many schools, leaders have misunderstood their role, disempowering some to give power to others, and seeking to have "democracy" by reaching for consensus on even the most basic of issues. Though the process is well intentioned, the time that is invested often saps the energies of the participants and consequently reduces rather than enhances the effectiveness of both the organization and the individuals themselves. Wheel spinning behavior exhausts and frustrates the organization's forward movement.

This caution leads us to a set of guidelines.

Top Ten Tips For Today's Leaders

I. Designated leaders must exercise strength and not apologize for it.

Schools must have key people who are in touch with the complexities of the enterprise and are empowered to act in the best interests of the people and the organization itself. There is a basic need for key decision-makers. A personal anecdote supports that idea.

Over twenty years ago, on the first day as a Columbia University Administrative Intern, Dr. Alden Larson, the Superintendent of Schools, called me aside and said..."Joe, as my Administrative Assistant you will be called upon to do many tasks. But be aware of the non-written aspect of your job description. You will be an ***administrative fender***."
"What's that?" I asked.
"That's someone who catches all the dirt that the big wheels throw around."

Schools do need a fender, a buffer to deflect the pressure and mud that inevitably gets thrown about. Teachers deserve the opportunity to conduct their classes in a safe and orderly environment. There has to be an insulation (not isolation) for the instructional program to be conducted properly. Call it security, or safety, even protectionism, the pa/maternalistic model has considerable validity. Fenders do need to exist to deflect and correct the strange things that occur in every school.

Reprinted with permission of Ford Button.

The fenders of organizations enable people to function safely in the workplace. Additionally if our fenders are really good at their leadership craft they can even avoid being like the character in Ford Button's cartoon!

II. Those engaged in the decision-making process should know the specific level of involvement they can operate within.

We run into trouble in organizations when we fail to clearly delineate the range of involvement of those who will be engaged in reaching decisions. Hagar once again offers enlightenment.

A perfectly logical question and a seemingly clear response. "Helga, you choose!" (It's o.k. with me. I'll go along with your decision and/or I don't want to decide.) Neat. Simple. Right? Wrong!! Check how this graphic unfolds.

Reprinted with special permission of King Features Syndicate, Inc.

A ha! The seemingly clear direction of "You choose" now has a different slant to it. Our Viking friend in essence says "You choose, but I had better agree with your choice!"

If leadership is to be shared then clear ground rules need to be established. If Hagar had said "Why don't we discuss some possibilities; then *we* can decide." Or, "I'll decide, but what are your thoughts?" Then war in the household might be avoided.

Designated leaders often fall into the trap of reversing decisions when committees reach consensus and the decision is at variance from what the administration wanted. Reversing a decision creates ill feeling and discourages people from collaboratively contributing to future efforts. Old animosities die hard. Though people can recognize specific lines of authority, processes that are ill defined blur areas of responsibility. We must pursue ways to sharpen our participatory processes.

Clarity results when people know the specifics upfront. **LEVELS of IN-VOLVEMENT** enables staff and committees to achieve far more effective participation. They range from lowest involvement to highest.

    • **Non-Involvement** (eg: Determining the *number* of fire drills to hold each year. The number is established by law and policy. You may ask and/or inform staff of the best time of day for a drill but determining the *number* of fire drills is not a group decision or shared process.)

    • **"I've made my decision...what do you think?"** (This enables the decision maker to see how a concept might fly and to determine if adjustments need be made.)

    • **"I will be making my decision...what do you think?"** (This says that others could have some influence on your decision. However you *retain* control.)

• **"Here is a situation or problem, come up with an answer, subject to my review."** (Basically this is what Hagar initially *meant*, but did not say.)

• **"Here is a situation or problem...solve it."** (And let me know how I may help.)

• **Identify your issues. Resolve/implement them.** (This one has the greatest latitude and corporate responsibility. The agenda is set and the decisions are made by the group.)

Ideally, prior to engaging in a task people will know what level of involvement they can function within. Though at times groups exceed their boundaries, more often than not they are comfortable working within clearly established limits. Clarifying the level of involvement helps define a group's participation and responsibility and enhances leadership.

III. Remember you can't be all things to all people.

The inner satisfaction from a job well done is known to all of us. Yet our designated leaders (a la Captain Marvel and Wonder Woman in Chapter 3) often try to do it all themselves. They are driven to gain the approval of all – an impossibility.

While high energy levels are typical of most leaders, many run the risk of doing much more than their fair share. It goes with the territory. And doing too much often means expending tremendous amounts of time in satisfying the need to know and influence everything!

In addition leaders can't be in touch with *all* that occurs in their domain. This ties in with the perfectionistic tendencies discussed in the third chapter. The following fable which is a paraphrased children's story may hit home.

...Owl lived alone in a hollow two story tree.

...Connecting the levels were a set of old worn stairs which were used by generations of owls long before.

... Now Owl was a perfectionist. He needed to know what was happening at all times in his home.

...When Owl was on the first level (the downstairs) he yearned to know what was happening upstairs... and,

...When Owl was on the second level (the upstairs) he yearned to know what was happening downstairs.

...Upstairs, he would call downstairs..."What's happening down there?"

...Downstairs, he would call upstairs..."What's happening up there?"

...He never heard an answer!

...Frustrated, Owl decided to run upstairs as fast as he could so he could know what was happening in both places. Yet when he got there and he called to the other level...no one answered.

...Faster and faster ran Owl...a blur of motion. Still no one answered.

...Faster and faster still ran Owl so that the leaves outside his home rustled in the wind. Still no one answered, and the only sounds he heard were of his breathing and the rustling leaves of his tree.

...Finally, following one last burst of energy, Owl collapsed on the middle step of his home...not knowing what was happening on either level and completely exhausted from the ordeal that he had put himself through.

Some leaders are like Owl. They need to know everything and in so doing exhaust themselves in the process. Are you like that?

Effective leaders empower others to act in support of a course that both find worthy. *Involvement in the process* is important to the success of a venture so leaders need to involve others in the process leading up to the decision. Successful leaders know that they are not omniscient, they are human and can only know and do so much.

IV. Leaders need to be aware of their own needs and leadership style to avoid unconsciously creating problems.

You may have worked for leaders whose actions seemed counter-productive to the development of the organization. You know the type – controlling, insecure – those who seek to limit the initiative of others so that they can manipulate and orchestrate issues and outcomes. At times, their style is consciously conducted; sometimes not. Let's review the former style.

I once worked for a superintendent who purposely kept people off-center to create, as he called it, "dynamic tension." Perhaps his thinking was that like water, people who are complacent tend to follow the easiest course – downhill. We never knew his goals. He shared little. Most wanted to avoid him, so few ever asked why he did what he did. Sad, but true.

While complacency is indeed something to avoid, creating dysfunctional situations just to keep people on their toes is inexcusable. Roman arbiter, Gaius Petronius, 66 A.D., had some thoughts on this type of leadership.

We trained hard – but it seemed that every time we formed into teams, we would be reorganized. I was to later learn that we tend to meet any new situation by reorganizing. And what a wonderful method it can be for creating the illusion of progress while producing confusion, inefficiency, and demoralization.

Secure, confident colleagues who are encouraged to move forward, to grow, to create, are essential components of an effective school or organization. Assessing our own needs and leadership style can enhance growth and avoid counterproductive behavior.

Contrast that superintendent's style with the type proposed by Britain's former Prime Minister, Harold Macmillan:

You must be like an oak tree – your branches spreading out widely so that new saplings may grow in your shade. You must not be a beech tree, growing so straight that you give no shade to the next generation.

Being in touch with your leadership style and professional motivators can increase your ability to guide others. Self-aware leaders employ some of the following strategies to increase their effectiveness.

STRATEGY #1. Insulate your hot buttons. Remember not to take others' behavior personally. To do so is to lose your objectivity. A clear focus is essential.

STRATEGY #2. Identify various personality types and establish a plan to help them develop their skills. Keeping in mind that difference can be a real asset to an organization, effective leaders set aside their stereotypes and develop plans to enhance the growth of their colleagues – *all colleagues.* This objectivity helps leaders create a positive balance in the organization.

STRATEGY #3. Motivate people to grow and change. Reinforcing teamwork while refusing to indulge negative behavior brings results. The "squeaky wheel" squeaks louder when reinforced. Accenting positives while quietly dealing with problems enhances the growth of all. "Keeping the ball in the air" (a la Denis Waitley and the volleyball story in Chapter 5) through conscious planning is within the grasp of every effective leader.

STRATEGY #4. Remember the notion of alterable variables. *Lord grant me the serenity to accept the things I cannot change, the courage to change the things I can, and the wisdom to know the difference.* This prayer of St. Francis of Assisi presents a powerful message. An *alterable variable* is one that can be influenced or changed – and that's where we should put our efforts. Balancing your checkbook will give you an accurate look at a piece of financial data. Then you can influence decisions about *your spending.* Balancing the national economy is obviously beyond your capacity and influence. It is an *unalterable variable* for you. Realize that some situations may be beyond your range of influence. Knowing which situations you can improve and which will defy your best efforts, can help you work smarter – not work harder.

Leaders need to experience success. Picking solvable issues enables us to build a good track record so that when we miss some tough ones, as we will, we've got a whole batch of positives in our personal archives to lean on. We don't have to live in the past, although after a particularly daring challenge we may need to think back to a time when the sun shone brightly.

V. Leaders need to avoid the "if" word.

"*If* only we had more money" "*If* our kids had scored higher on those state tests"...*if, if, if*. Wallowing in the murky bog of regrets, blaming others, or inventing alibis are destructive to leaders' credibility and performance. Close the door on matters that are over and done with. Your time as a leader needs to be devoted to present and future functioning rather than being a "past dweller." Looking ahead improves leadership.

VI. Know and use cardinal rules for resolving conflict with others.

Organizational fenders are necessary to catch the mud because mud does happen in any organization. Although the ideas presented below should not be viewed as a cookbook, they do represent validated practices that enable leaders to remain focused on the resolution of difficulties. They presume that the parties in a disagreement wish to resolve an issue. If the parties seek to prolong the conflict for the sake of the conflict itself, then the leader as mediator may have no choice but to disengage from the situation as a means of momentarily handling it. Since most people want to avoid conflict, these rules may be applied with an expectation of success.

- Share an empathetic comment to set the tone for your interaction (e.g.: "I'm glad we have this opportunity to talk because I am fully optimistic that within the next 20 minutes we will have made progress in the resolution of your concern.")

- Be concrete and specific. Identify the issue at hand. State that resolution is in the best interests of all. Identify a common interest to the parties (e.g.: wanting a student's behavior or grades to improve).

- Deal with but one issue at a time. Stay with that topic before you move on.

- When you state the problem, immediately suggest a solution; avoid harping on the problem.

- Recognize that the solution should be a specific behavior in the future.

- Respondent's first reponsibility is to listen and give feedback.

- If not agreeing with the solution, the respondent shall suggest another specific behavioral solution.

- Focus on behavioral change, not ideational change.

- Changing topics takes place only with mutual consent.

- Continue the process of suggesting solutions until both parties mutually agree on one.

- Don't be reluctant to take a time out if an acceptable solution is not forthcoming. Reschedule a session to resolve the matter. If you are attempting to resolve conflict as a third party, set the meeting and establish your expectation that closure/resolution will occur by the end of your next session. Very often it will be resolved even before the scheduled meeting is to take place.

- "Check out" the agreement or plan of action. Make sure that all parties are aware of what has occurred.

- At all costs, avoid sarcasm, harping, personal attacks, crystal ball gazing and off-task behavior.

- Remember it is best to promote
  - same day clearance of issues
  - frequent pauses to evaluate the situation and/or solutions
  - direct, warm, business-like behavior.

VII. Introspectively analyze your strengths, weaknesses, and biases.

Perhaps that negative superintendent referred to earlier could have been much more productive if he had been in touch with the following introspective questions and had seriously answered them.

- Does my action(s) support our organization's cause, rather than my ego, emotion or opinion?

- Will my action(s) empower those around me to make more complete decisions?

- Will my action(s) encourage positive thinking?

- Am I proactive in seeking solutions, or do I perpetuate the problem?

- Am I and do I project understanding, support and problem solving? How?

- Do I truly value others. How do I project these feelings?

- Do I laugh? Am I flexible?

- By my behavior, do I basically serve as a model of authenticity for others?

As a leader you might want to develop your own set of questions and periodically review them. Getting to the heart of **YOU** is important to the success of your school. Remember leaders are significant, and they influence everything of significance in the organization.

VIII. Use humor to showcase and enhance your humanity.

Leaders carry a different type of union card. They often haul around the extra weight of some prestige, status and role whether earned or not. Many leaders become detached from the group as a consequence of these extra burdens. Separation from the "troops" is not always consciously done. At times our roles, and job performance tend to head us away from others. Leaders need to remain credible and capable during times of estrangement. Relating to others on the trivia level is important to leaders' approachability.

If you want to remain connected or reconnect with colleagues, try this simple technique.

Laughter is like glue – it connects people in positive ways

USE LAUGHTER, especially at yourself; it lets others know that you don't take yourself too seriously. While there are times that a leader, like Rodney Dangerfield, "gets no respect," self-deprecating humor does indeed bring respect. It comforts people to know that those in positions of authority are not all powerful and don't regard themselves as such. Remember angels fly because they take themselves lightly! When people are confident enough to joke about themselves, the group will usually respect those individuals even more. Try it – but watch your timing and don't overdo it. Moderation is important. Noel Coward advised, "Wit ought to be a glorious treat, like caviar; never spread about like marmalade." Morris Udall in his book, *Too Funny To Be President* (1988), contends that to laugh at oneself is "a healthy antidote for a suffocating sense of self-importance."

Thomas Werge, Professor of English at Notre Dame University, has studied humor and its many ramifications (1990). By emphasizing that laughter can be a tremendously powerful tool and by referencing Udall's intentions, Werge contends that "...humor has the ability to restore perspective, remind us to take work seriously (but not ourselves) and to provide light and balance amid excruciatingly self-important seers, pundits and grand viziers." He cites Peter DeVries' comments on the ultimate fate of our self-importance and vanity..."We are all like the cleaning lady. We all come to dust!"

Beware of biting sarcasm which leaves bitterness in its wake. Good natured humor that is rooted in a spirit of love and decency gets much greater results. Leaders who capitalize on the moment, provide others with a forum to display their senses of humor, and who share the joy of their own laughter are among the most revered and respected. And, perhaps the most effective as well. A few examples may help us to practice what we preach.

Perspectives on Leadership...

The trouble with being a leader today is that you can't be sure whether people are following you, or chasing you!

Reprinted with permission of Frank Cotham

"We have no leader here – just our principal, Mr. Langburn."

Remember what the mama whale told the baby whale: When you get to the top and start letting off steam, that's the time when you're most likely to get harpooned!

The higher a person climbs, the more his rear is exposed.

- Vinegar Joe Stillwell

HAGAR DIK BROWNE

Reprinted with special permission of King Features Syndicate, Inc.

On our significance as leaders...

> *Sometimes when you feel that your going*
> *Would leave an unfillable hole.*
> *Just follow this simple suggestion*
> *And see how it humbles your soul.*
>
> *Take a bucket and fill it with water,*
> *Put your hand in it up to the wrist,*
> *Pull it out – and the hole that's remaining*
> *Is a measure of how you'll be missed.*
>
> *You may splash all you please when you enter,*
> *You can stir up the water galore,*
> *But stop, and you'll find in a minute*
> *That it looks quite the same as before.*

– Author unknown

IX. Communicate, communicate, communicate

Someone once said that the leader who gets the most satisfactory results is not always the person with the most brilliant mind, but rather the one who can best coordinate the brains and talents of others. In order to serve in a coordinative fashion, leaders need to know what is going on as well as to share what's happening on their turf. (But be leary of the "Owl Syndrome.")

The process of developing and sharing a vision is enhanced through effective communications. Many leaders are intuitively strong in this area. However, all can benefit from a thoughtful approach. In the effective school we communicate on differing levels. We do so not only with words but through our attitudes and actions. In the first chapter, the communications mountain, was presented.

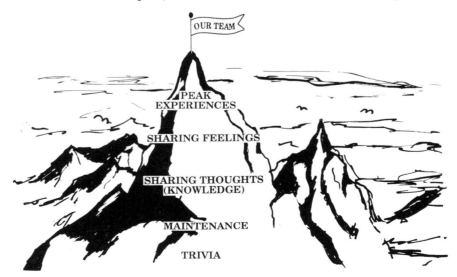

Briefly recapping...we establish safe linkages with our colleagues on the *trivia* level; deal with the structure and efficiency of our organizations at the *maintenance* level; *share knowledge* as we climb higher and explore new learnings; *share feelings* when we evaluate and head toward substantive decisions, and occasionally achieve *peak experiences* when we are as one in our communications. Though each level has a set of conditions and variables, the developmental nature of climbing the "mountain" to reach the top is well within the ability of leaders to understand and create.

Effective communications is a critical part of a leader's repertoire of skills. Attention to the following may hone those skills:

Ten Commandments of Communication

1 - Identify the level within which you wish to communicate

While we often seize the moment to touch base with colleagues during our busy days, people are often disarmed when levels are mixed. For example, a light conversation on the *trivia* level, should not be elevated to the *sharing feelings* level unless both parties are comfortable in doing so. "Pavement" conferences enable us to quickly share information. In-depth communications take time and planning.

2 - Know why you are communicating

Before you communicate ask yourself what you wish to accomplish with your message. Do you wish to gain or share information, get the ball rolling on a project or lay the groundwork for a change in a person's outlook? Be careful to limit the scope of your communication – the narrower or sharper the focus the greater the chance of success.

3 - Crystalize your thoughts before you communicate

The more carefully you analyze your subject, the more you can get to the heart of the topic you wish to convey. Planning is essential. Good planning takes into account the attitudes of those with whom you are communicating and your own objectives for the interaction. Good communication takes effort, especially as you operate on the higher levels of the mountain.

4 - Convey something of value in your communications

Ever heard of the radio station W.I.I.F.M. (What's in it for me)? Many leaders fail to assess that people are most reponsive when the message is of personal importance. Using examples that pertain to your colleagues, their classes, and their experiences or interests heightens interest in what you have to say.

5 - Be sensitive to your delivery

Your body language, tone of voice, facial expression, preoccupation with other thoughts, and distractability all have a significant bearing on how your message is received. *How you present* your message is almost as important as what you have to say. Be approachable, maintain eye contact, be open, use positive body language, and your message will be welcomed.

In racing from point A to point B in the course of a busy day, pause, take a breath, and set aside other pressures when trying to communicate with others. Have you heard "I didn't want to bother you, you're so busy?" We need to convey to others that during this moment in time our dialogue is the most important thing on our mind. Leaders, busy as they actually are, don't always take the time to communicate that notion to their colleagues.

6 - Consider the setting

We must be sensitive not only about the level on which we are communicating, but to the location and circumstances as well. We shouldn't transmit sensitive information where it imposes on another's space.   Sharing a performance suggestion with a supervisor over lunch, when others are at the table or within earshot makes it awkward for your colleagues; even if it may not be a problem for you and your supervisor. This is common sense, but how often do we violate it?

7 - Effective communications require follow up

A new social studies teacher was shocked to learn of the poor end-of-year test results of his students. Investigating, it was discovered that he assumed that he had taught his course material well initially, so that a review was not necessary. Wrong.   Leaders often make the same mistake. When communications are reinforced through follow-up notes, minutes, updates in weekly bulletins, etc. the messages become internalized.

8 - Consult with others

When you plan a communication or ascertain facts upon which to develop it, it is helpful to involve others. They not only will broaden your knowledge, but will share perceptions that can clarify or reinforce your message. Colleagues may also be more objective about the topic than you might be.

9 - Communicate for tomorrow and make sure that your actions support your communications

Much of our communications deal with the present and are designed to avoid past problems. Yet we must be mindful of presenting growth opportunities and maintaining connections with long range objectives. The leader who identifies a problem and promptly detaches from any involvement in its resolution, encourages others to do the same. The principal who makes an impassioned plea for staff to periodically check the lavatories to discourage student loitering, and who doesn't personally follow-up as a member of the "potty patrol" will more often than not find that few staff members follow through. Substance begets substance.

10- Listen, listen, listen

Listening is one of the most demanding, most important, and often most neglected skills in communications. It demands that we concentrate not only on what the person is expressing (explicit meaning) but on gestures, unspoken words, and undertones (implicit meanings). We listen more frequently than any other activity. Statistics indicate that unless we have been trained as listeners, we retain only 25% of what we hear. It is further indicated that 60% of all misunderstandings relate to hearing/listening. Contrast that figure with 1% due to visual misunderstanding.

So what can leaders do to improve listening skills? Sean Joyce (1985) provides some helpful hints in *The Management Workshop.*

To Be A Better Listener You Should

• Mentally recapitulate about every five minutes as you listen. It takes about five seconds to do and more than doubles the probability of understanding and retention.

• In one to one sessions recapitulate orally; play back to the speaker what you believe you've heard. When off center you can correct it. When on target you can reinforce it. Say it in your own words. Include a bit of what you believe the other person is feeling. But be careful not to parrot back; that can be annoying. Give the other a chance to verify your paraphrasing.

• Identify the key points/building blocks inherent in the speaker's message. Once again summarize them and/or play them back.

• Establish a reason, purpose or goal for listening. (e.g.: to form an opinion, to learn something new, to obtain news, to discover a speaker's attitude.)

• In person to person communications use Robert Montgomery's LADD formula:

> L - Look at the person you are speaking with. Attention enhances the importance of your discussion.
> A - Ask questions.
> D - Don't interrupt. It is just as rude to step on ideas as on toes.
> D - Don't change the subject or get into "one-upmanship." Give the other the chance for his due.

To Montogmery's LADD add Hoff's COYE – *Clean Out Your Ears*, (your predispositions toward the other person). Prejudgments are one of the biggest roadblocks to effective communications and listening.

Each of us needs to develop concentrated listening skills. Leaders who wish to increase their effectiveness can do so in dramatic fashion by taking the time, closing their mouths, and opening their perceptions. Bernard Baruch's admonition is applicable:

You can win more friends in two months by showing interest in other people than you can in two years by trying to interest others in yourself.

LISTEN

When I ask you to listen to me
and you start giving advice
you have not done what I ask.

When I ask you to listen to me
and you begin to tell me why I shouldn't feel that way,
you are trampling on my feelings.

Listen! All I asked was that you listen; not talk or do;
just hear me.

Advice is cheap; 30 cents will get you both Dear Abby and
Billy Graham in the same newspaper.

And I can do for myself; I'm not helpless.
Maybe discouraged and faltering, but not helpless.

When you do something for me that I can and need to do for
myself, you contribute to my fear and weakness.

But, when you accept as a simple fact that I do feel that I feel,
no matter how irrational, then I can quit trying to convince you
and can get about the business of understanding
what's behind this irrational feeling.

And when that's clear, the answers are obvious
and I don't need advice.

Irrational feelings make sense when we understand what's
behind them.

Perhaps that's why prayer works, sometimes, for some people
because God is mute, and He doesn't give advice or try to fix things.
"They" just listen and let you work it out for yourself.

So, please listen and just hear me. And if you want to
talk, wait a minute for your turn; and,

I'll listen to you.

– Author unknown

X. "Role" your own

Paraphrasing the old cigarette smoker's admonition, this one is yours to create.Develop #10 as your own. Doing so may put you in a creative frame of mind so that you could develop your own Top Ten. Meeting this challenge depends on conscious thought about the models that you select as your guides, the circumstances you work within, and the wonderful composite of what you are.

As a leader, you need to develop your guiding principles and use them as benchmarks. If you wish, you might draw them from the nine key leadership tasks...*(Envision Goals, Affirm Values, Motivate, Manage, Achieve a Workable Level of Unity, Explain, Serve as a Role Model, Represent the Group Externally, and Renew...by continually growing and learning.)*

———————————●———————————

The first two-thirds of the chapter dealt with the individual dimension of leadership. We found that effective leaders who captured the imagination of everyone in their organizations provided time to communicate; validated and listened to others; established clear parameters within which decisions were made; and conveyed a high degree of single-mindedness and dedication to an agenda for the future.

Effective leaders by the very definition of their role must be adept in working with people; people who possess a wide range of interests, talents and needs. Leaders must have an inner calm and confidence – call it self-esteem, thick skin, or talent. Whatever or however it is categorized, the leader needs to have an ability to detach and retreat to the central core of a healthful perspective. To that end, one touchstone warrants sharing. It deals with the inner strength and confidence one must have in enacting a leadership role, especially when times get tough.

> *If I were to read, much less answer all the attacks made on me, this shop might well be closed for any other business. I do the best I know how, the very best I can; I mean to keep on doing it to the end. If the end brings me out all right, what is said against me will not amount to anything. If the end brings me out all wrong, 10 angels swearing I was right would make no difference.*
>
> *– Abraham Lincoln*

(This quotation mounted on a wooden plaque was given to Winston Churchill by Franklin Delano Roosevelt who kept it in his study at Chartwell.)

American organizations face major tests and challenges to change. Just as the post World War II market dominance of American technology has been challenged by the competition of regional, multi-national and global corporations, previous patterns of leadership have been tested and scrutinized. While it can be argued that American industry failed to remain competitive, there are multiple factors that went into creating the shift in balance. One weakness was in the type of planning industry used.

There are basically two types of planning. *Linear* planning occurs when you are stationary and try to hit a moving target. Most year-long planning in schools is of this variety. *Strategic* planning is when you are in motion and try to hit a moving target. It involves looking at your organization, conducting an analysis and examining the future. Making adjustments in a unit teaching plan under way or totally shifting your direction to reflect knowledge learned or not learned in a day's lesson by the students, is an example of this variety. The latter implies an organization in motion and a plan that addresses variables that change constantly. The former implies that once you've set your plan you start up the train and you remain on the tracks until you reach your goal. Linear planning too often gathers dust. Curriculum guides tend to be linear in their design.

Strategic planning assumes that though you target certain outcomes, you do not lose sight of the plan or the many variables that have or could have an impact on your targets. This type of plan becomes well worn with many adaptations along the way. Both industry and the schools need to do more with strategic rather than linear planning. Good teachers inherently know this fact – yet many schools do not.

Participatory leadership in order to be effective must avoid being static. While the basic structure of a plan needs to be well defined, flexibility that comes from responding to changing variables must be inherent in the plan. Shared leadership for an organization that is in motion is natural. Shared leadership for an organization that is static can shake the bedrock foundations of its existence.

Soren Kierkegaard in discussing the ambivalence of standing on your own two feet said:

> *The loving mother teaches her child to walk alone. She is far enough from him so that she cannot actually support him. She holds out her arms. Her face beckons like a reward, an encouragement. The child constantly strives toward a refuge in her embrace, little suspecting that in the very same moment he is emphasizing his need for her, he is proving that he can do without her.*

That quote has an undeniable ring of truth. In organizations that are vibrant, the development of new structures of governance and shared decision making become as natural as the child breaking free from the mother, but returning when nurturance is needed or desired. The principal's security and ability to "let go" factors heavily in the development of shared leadership activities. Keep in mind that leadership in an organization can be static or in motion.

The contemporary principalship is buffeted by resource shortages, decaying autonomy, and conflicting requirements. Burnout is a growing phenomenon that causes incalculable harm to principals' lives and significant disruption to their organizations. Principals have acquired so many differing responsibilities that they rarely recognize that their "job jar" runneth over to the degree that many no longer can keep up. Just as "real men don't eat quiche," real principals hesitate in acknowledging the fact that they are overwhelmed.

The following rather jaundiced view, but one that typifies the traditional role of management, was attributed to the former chief executive officer of International Harvester, John L. McCaffrey.

> *As nearly everyone knows, an executive has practically nothing to do, except to decide what is to be done; to tell somebody to do it; to listen to reasons why it should not be done, why it should be done by someone else, or why it should be done in a different way; to follow up to see if the thing has been done; to discover that it has been done incorrectly; to point out how it should have been done; to conclude that as long as it has been done, it may as well be left where it is; to wonder if it is not time to get rid of a person who cannot do a thing right; to reflect that he probably has a wife and a large family, and that certainly any successor would be just as bad, and may be worse; to consider how much simpler and better the thing would have been done if one had done it oneself in the first place; to reflect sadly that one could have done it in twenty minutes, and as things turn out, one has to spend two days to find out why it has taken three weeks for someone else to do it wrong.*

I'm not certain if McCaffrey was saying this seriously or tongue in cheek. But if taken seriously, most would have a great deal of trouble accepting this negative mindset.

In our awakenings as empowered organizations, the development of a logical course of leadership is to engage people in the ownership and operation of their schools. The boss at International Harvester needed to be in touch with participatory leadership issues as a counter point to his skewed logic. Katheryn E. Nelson (1979) articulated her awakenings at a National Leadership Conference in this piece titled *A Leader*.

A LEADER

I went on a search to become a leader.

I searched high and low. I spoke with authority and people listened but alas, there was one who was wiser than I and they followed him.

I sought to inspire confidence but the crowd responded, "Why should we trust you?"

I postured and I assumed the look of leadership with a countenance that flowed with confidence and pride. But many passed me by and never noticed my air of elegance.

I ran ahead of the others, pointing the way to new heights. I demonstrated that I knew the route to greatness. And then I looked back and I was alone.

What shall I do, I queried? I've tried hard and used all that I know.

And I sat me down and I pondered long.

And then I listened to the voices around me. And I heard what the group was trying to accomplish.

I rolled up my sleeves and joined in the work.

As we worked I asked, "Are we all together in what we want to do and how to get the job done?"

And we thought together and we fought together and we struggled toward our goal.

I found myself encouraging the fainthearted. I sought the ideas of those too shy to speak out.

I taught those who had little skill. I praised those who worked hard.

When our task was completed, one of the groups turned to me and said, "This would not have been done but for your leadership."

At first I said, "I didn't lead, I just worked with the rest."

And then I understood: leadership is not a goal. It's a way of reaching a goal.

I lead best when I help others to go where we've decided we want to go.

I lead best when I help others to use themselves creatively.

I lead best when I forgot about myself as leader and focused on my group, their needs and their goals.

To lead is to serve. To give – to achieve TOGETHER.

– Katheryn E. Nelson

Nelson discovered that the primary attribute of those who would lead is the support and assistance they give to others. Essential is the capacity of the leaders to know where the group is going and to invite and subtly influence others to join them on the voyage.

Leaders should make a habit of seeking the involvement of others, because nobody is infallible. The Elizabethan playwright, Ben Johnson, wrote "No man is so wise that he may not easily err if he takes no other counsel but his own."

It would appear to be self-defeating not to seek advice wherever possible. When Nelson gave up her "air of elegance" and "listened to the voices around her" she became a part of the group and her leadership capacity surfaced. The distinquished English preacher, John Balguy (1738), supported this premise in these words.

> *Whoever is wise is apt to suspect and be diffident of himself, and upon that account is willing to harken into council; whereas the foolish man, being in proportion to his folly, full of himself, and swallowed up in conceit, will seldom take any counsel but his own, and for the very reason that it is his own.*

Each person fits into the empowered school. Each leader helps the pieces come together.

A participatory leader seeks the advice of others and in the process is able to share in kind. As discussed in Chapter 5, leaders trust others with their fate just as they expect the trust of others in return. With this connectedness, leaders possess power and are able to "stay the course" even when others around them falter. Their relatedness serves both as a guide for others and a personal source of strength.

Dependence, co-dependence, interdependence are important to the development of a sense of *organizational security* in an empowered leadership design. Here's an illustration of that point:

> *The story is told that the captain of a large cargo ship and the chief engineer were constantly squabbling. Each criticized the other as they argued which was more essential to the welfare of the ship. One day after yet another disagreement, they decided to swap places.*
>
> *The captain descended to the boiler room while the chief climbed to the bridge. After a few hours the captain returned to the bridge covered with oil and grease.*
>
> *"Chief!" he exclaimed while wildly waving aloft a huge monkey wrench. "You'll have to return to the boiler room, I can't make her go!"*
>
> *"Of course, you can't," replied the chief. "I've just run aground!"*

Interdependence...with very important yet differing responsibilities to the ship creates *security* when people can depend on the talents and functioning of others. *Trust* helps considerably.

The chapter began with the strong belief that: *Teachers* are *leaders* and *principals* are leaders of *leaders*. Former C.E.O. McCaffrey's "owlish" remarks (racing to the different levels of his tree to find out what was happening out there) reaffirm the need for trust and a "leader among leaders" mindset. Effective principals know that they can rely more on "referent"power (personal relationships) and "expert"power (technical knowledge and skills) than on "positional" power (*I am the principal!*) to get things done. Effective principals know that the job is being done quite well by others and that their subtle encouragement will motivate people to do an even better job in the future. Leaders who are in touch with the research also know such principles as the following.

• Leadership is specific to a situation – accordingly different people are leaders in different situations.

• Leadership is a group characteristic – and depends on interaction and interdependence (as in the cargo ship story).

• Some common traits or qualities demonstrated by most leaders are initiative, empathy, creativity, cooperation, hard work, energy, knowledgeability, and helpfulness to others.

• Principals who are effective have a clearly formulated and articulated school vision or mission, focus their goals on student learning, create a safe and orderly environment, provide strong instructional leadership, initiate and facilitate change, are good speakers, listen, and are sympathetic and decisive.

• Leadership is diverse and most people are leaders in some activity.

• Group decisions under trained leaders are more effective than those under untrained leaders.

• School principals are usually reluctant to communicate with others about the things they do.

Leaders who are in touch with the art of leadership also know that their role is instrumental in changing (guiding/supporting) a group's focus from what is to what can be. Leaders know that sharing with others gives others the encouragement to share with them as well. This practice when not overdone helps to shape the character of the group. Principals need to share the dynamic nature of their responsibilities. Catching each other leading, teaching and learning builds an inter-related trusting relationship. The chief engineer and captain are both essential to the success of a voyage.

A simple experiment illustrates the best way to influence the direction in which people head. Take a loose piece of string 4-6" long. Place it on the table. Pull it and it will follow wherever you wish it to go. Return it to the table. Push it and it tends to go nowhere at all. It bunches and defies direction. Gentle guiding rather than pushing yields desired movement.

Think of the traditional organizational chart on the wall of many business types. It is decorative and showy; it has order to it; it is neat and implies efficiency – but it gathers dust.

The chart implies that the organization is static. Lines of authority flow downward from a single entity and multiply as they go down. People report to one supervisor who reports to another who reports, etc. It implies that work flows neatly. It implies that the titles of people mean that *they alone* accomplish the discreet body of work that they do. It implies that bureaucracy is the norm and communication never skips a step;that people at the bottom are detached from those at the top,and that even on the horizontal line, job functions don't mesh.

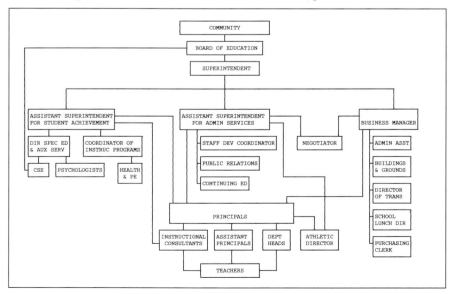

How unfortunate, how limiting, and how wrong. **Participatory leadership is a shared decision-making process.** Its success resides in the simple fact that people who share in the process will do a better job of implementing the resulting decision. Unlike the organizational wall chart, it provides for a broad range of involvement with a high degree of ownership for the decisions. It provides a means of recognizing everyone in the organization rather than allocating some to a lower slot in the pecking order of importance. It implies a shared commitment to responsibility and accountability as well.

Shared decision making does *not* involve the displacment or shuffling of administrative duties or ultimate responsibility. The effective administrator is an essential cog in the smoothly functioning wheel of the organization.

What participatory leadership does mean is that staff have input and make decisions in those areas that are germane to their operation. It allows for issues to be identified and acted upon from the bottom up as opposed to the top down.

When effective, it recognizes that levels of decision making exist and that all affected personnel take a role in assessing the problem and either recommending or taking a course of action.

Reprinted with permission of Bardulf Ueland

Organizational models of staff involvement in leadership and school-wide decision making

Though a variety of models exist in today's schools, there are basically five which command most of the research attention.

1. **Principal's Advisory Council (PAC)**
   The PAC is designed to improve the organizational climate and the effectiveness of the principal's decision making responsibility. This group is representational and when coupled with an understanding of "Levels of Participatory Involvement" can have a significant affect on the operation of the school. PAC assists in the dissemination of information at the building level and deals with issues on the *maintenance level* of the Communications Mountain.

2. **Instructional Support Team**

This team's main purpose is to improve instruction by increasing school-site leadership and teamwork between administration and staff. It usually concentrates on curricular concerns and student performance issues. The I.S.T. calls for representation/operation on the *sharing knowledge level*.

3. **School Improvement Team**

This team is a representational school-based council that deals with specific issues leading to improvement activities. Many schools involved in the Effective Schools movement use this forum to deal with specific correlates (safe & orderly environment, parent involvement, etc.) relating to the improvement of building performance levels. This team is involved in data driven decision making and operates primarily at the *maintenance* and *knowledge sharing levels*.

4. **School Based Management Council**

The Council oversees a school that operates by committee. The Council often has parent and student involvement. Major policy decisions concern this group. The chairperson is usually not the principal although a co-chair arrangement with the principal is not uncommon. Often referred to as site-based management, this group usually operates at the maintenance level although it can delve into higher levels via curricular issues.

5. **Lead Teacher Committee**

This committee is usually the result of a contractual agreement. It broadens accountability and extends leadership beyond the principal. Often the result of a situation where there has been a leadership void, the committee represents a radical change from the prevailing organizational pattern of today's schools. In situations where there has been organizational dysfunction, this committee is designed to augment or replace the principal's authority and replace it with a more effective model. Though conceptually this model exists to share leadership, decision making and responsibility, it has been quite controversial in its disempowerment of some to empower others. The effectiveness of this model has yet to be determined, as insufficient data exists. It too is designed to operate primarily at the *maintenance level* with incursions into *sharing knowledge* via curricular issues.

Note that these committees, councils, and teams have elements that overlap. All are representational, most operate on the *maintenance level*, and all are conceptually designed to broaden the base of involvement and decision making. The error of their design, if there is a flaw, is that most operate at the level which basically is the most efficient in our organizations – *maintenance*. It's like an adept school superintendent who guides a challenging board into non-substantive issues such as the cost of office supplies so that the administration has the latitude to deal with more professional issues in an unencumbered fashion.

Generally the most effective councils have been of the Instructional Support Team design. These councils get to the curricular meat of the school's purpose.

The ultimate purpose of school leadership is improved teaching and learning. The School Improvement Team model tends toward that loftier range of functioning but all too often teams get mired in nuts and bolts administrative issues. (Please note that the full range – *trivia* to *peak experience levels* may be engaged by all groups. The preponderant functioning level is what has been generalized for each council.) Each council develops its own personality and varies greatly from school to school. The basic responsibility for carrying out any recommendations remains, of course, with the principal.

Remember the cynical one-liner, "In a democracy, people are free to choose the person who'll get the blame!" When something goes wrong, central administration will seek the principal for explaining it and correcting it. There are exceptions; for instance, curricular decisions are usually referred back to the council or committee. But when test scores are not up to desired standards, who is sought – the principal of course. In its design, shared decision making and participatory involvement carry *accountability for the group* as well as for the designated building leader – but it doesn't work out that way as yet. Some good beginnings, however, may yet lead to corporate responsibility and ownership.

In developing your model make sure that it is in pursuit of shared objectives. Reorganization can often be a smoke screen to get at substantive concerns; inefficient communications, firing incompetent administrators, making tough budgetary conditions seem more palatable and basically "stirring the pot" for the sake of...stirring the pot! In developing your school's model make sure your focus is clear and above board.

Success in developing a team approach depends on the attitude you bring to the table. Roger Von Oech (1986) has a great deal to share on perceptions in his book, *A Kick In The Seat Of The Pants*. Here is an example.

> *Take a look around where you're sitting and find five things that have blue in them. Go ahead and do it. With a "blue" mindset, you'll find that blue jumps out at you: a blue book on the table, a blue pillow on the couch, blue in the painting on the wall, and so on. Similarly, whenever you learn a new word, you hear it six times in the next two days. In like fashion, you've probably noticed that after you buy a new car, you promptly see that make of car everywhere. That's because people find what they are looking for. If you're looking for conspiracies, you'll find that too. It's all a matter of setting your mental channel (p. 27).*

No matter what plan you develop or are investigating – go in with the mind set of catching people at their very best. Your council will get off the ground smashingly when, as Von Oech suggests, you set your mental channel properly.

All too often we take something simple and make it complex. But to take something that's complex and make it simple, that's creativity. Simple isn't always easy as this Will Rogers story points out.

> *During World War II, Rogers was prone to give simple answers to complex issues. He had a suggestion for getting rid of the German submarines. Said Rogers..."All we have to do is heat up the Atlantic to 212 °F, then the subs will have to surface and we can pick them off one by one. Now, somebody's going to want to know how to warm up the ocean. Well, I'm not going to worry about that. It's a matter of detail and I'm a policy maker.*

In empowered schools, all are policy makers. In order to expand the base of leadership and decision making, unlike Rogers, we need to concern ourselves with details...

> the details of our trust...
> the details of our interdependence...
> the details of our role intersections...
> the details of our teamwork...
> the details of our individual and group leadership skills,
>   and...
> the details of the development of our organizations into the
>   *Best Places They Can Be –*
> *Because We Have the Wit to Make It So!*

Keep in mind that organizational shared decision making may be initially as fragile as a butterfly's wing, yet in the capable hands of sensitive leaders, empowerment can soar to new heights of accomplishment.

Chapter 8 both synthesizes the seven preceeding chapters and also offers many practical tips that you can apply to "The Enabling Environment" of your empowered school.

Chapter 8
Pulling It All Together: The Enabling Environment

A young boy walked along a stretch of beach skimming shells into the waves. The boy noticed the distant figure of an old man. Curious to see what the man was doing, he dropped his shells and ran through the sand.

As he approached, the boy noticed the man repeatedly stooping to pick up objects and throw them beyond the breaking surf. The boy also noticed that the sand was strewn with thousands of starfish, washed ashore by the outgoing tide. The boy watched the man repeat his actions of returning starfish to the cool waters before they became lifeless, baked by the noonday sun.

The boy spoke. "I see you throwing starfish into the ocean old man. Why are you doing that?"

"To make a difference," replied the man.

"Surely," said the boy, "with thousands of starfish all over the beach what possible difference could you make?"

The man smiled knowingly as he reached for yet another starfish. As he tossed it far from shore, he said. "It makes a difference to this one, son – it makes a difference to this one."

The boy left the old man and thought about his words. As he walked along the beach, once again alone, he began picking up objects – tossing them into the sea. However, instead of sea shells this time, they were starfish. The boy was returning them to their home. He learned a powerful lesson that day. The boy discovered that he too could make a difference.

In organizations, making a difference depends on the actions of each member. That mind-set takes conscious effort, that effort takes communications, communications leads to a common purpose, a common purpose leads to knowledge and understanding, and knowledge and understanding enables us to make a difference. And all of these elements require a safe, positive, nurturing **environment** in which people can securely function. The environment of the empowered school, like the actions and simple words of the old man, is a powerful teacher.

It is universally agreed that we need to intensify the effectiveness of all schools today. Those concerned with creating a better match between the personal and intellectual needs of our students and the effectiveness of the school need to create an environment that is supportive.

Characteristics of an Enabling Environment

• *Has well understood and effectively applied theoretical foundations of learning, teaching and communicating.*

A school in the Netherlands artistically captures students through plywood graphics.

• *Understands, appreciates, displays, and validates the worth of its students and staff.*

• *Has staff who are in touch with their motivators, needs, and professional patterns of interaction.*

• *Collaboratively involves people in the process of change.*

• *Periodically asks...Why are we doing what we're doing?...and utilizes past and present success as benchmarks for future accomplishments.*

• *Empowers all in planning, achieving and maintaining a synergized team.*

• *Recognizes that shared leadership increases ownership for decision making and organizational productivity.*

• *Is philosophically, visually, procedurally and aesthetically congruent with the purposes of the organization.*

• *Confidently creates the future.*

These conditions are, of course, the focus of the first seven chapters.

What then is the environment of an empowered school? It is not just the **culture** (the way we do business around here) or the **climate** (how we feel about what we do). The environment is the **setting** – the playing field if you will – in which all come to face the challenge of developing the finest collective enterprise possible. It is an **attitude**; one in which each and every starfish and those who reach out to help them are equally prized.

The environment is both a place and a state of mind where people come together to make a difference and create the future. The future capabilities and character of our students are most di-rectly influenced by the environment we create. Further on in the chapter, this concept will be illustrated by the enabling environment of Churchville-Chili Middle School located in Western New York State. Keep in mind that there is no such thing as only one type of enabling environment. Qualities that are unique to an organization provide the "character" of the organization. Each is different and though ideas may have a similar look, the character of schools is never the same.

As with people, schools have differ-ent personalities. In some the staff and students work together in a spirit of harmony. In others there is fragmen-tation, hostility, and little productiv-ity. The central purpose of any school is to provide the finest possible educa-tional program for its students. Each school is a "starfish" well worthy of our attention. But what occurs in the place we call school is often at odds with its own mission.

A turn of the century slate chalkboard has a message of welcome for all.

The following application exercises and examples which draw together the discussion of the first seven chapters may prove helpful in setting a clear vision for your empowered school.

———————•———————

1. THE ENABLING ENVIRONMENT is one that understands and effectively applies theoretical foundations of learning, teaching, and communicating. (Chapter 1)

Robert Fulghum, author of *All I Need to Know I Learned in Kindergarten,* developed a personal litany on eduation which was published in a special edition of *Newsweek, Fall/Winter 1990.* It is theory in an understandable form. His points are worth considering as they relate to an enabling environment.

- Learning is taking place at all times in all circumstances for every person.

- There are as many ways to learn something as there are people.

- There is no one way to learn anything – learn how you learn – help the student to do likewise.

- There is nothing everyone must know.

- All I have to do is accept the consequences of what I do not know.

- There is no one way to be human.

- Imagination is more important than information.

- The quality of education depends more on what's going on at home than in the school. And more on what is going on in the student than what is going on in the teacher.

- In learning, don't ask for food; ask for farming lessons. In teaching, vice versa.

- If nobody learns as much as the teacher, then turn students into teachers.

- Every student has something important to teach the teacher.

In Chapter 1 we spoke of learning triangles, and the connectedness that came from being confident enough about *that which I know* to apply our learning to real life situations. Maslow's needs hierarchy states that *human needs can be arranged in a hierarchy* and that before an individual can effectively contend with knowledge and understanding, he first has to have his physical needs, security and safety needs, love and belonging, and self-esteem needs met. Though a variety of instructional techniques is appropriate in the pyramid of learning, *the curve of retention is dramatically increased when students immediately apply their learning by teaching others* (The Learning Pyramid). And we discovered that in order to climb our organizational mountain to reach peak experiences, that we need to master different *stages of communications* (The Communications Mountain).

Fulghum centers on the notions that each is unique, all can learn, all can teach, and all are ultimately accountable for their learning. The Starfish Story is inherent in Fulghum's philosophy. The theme of making a difference through positive connections with learning theory was woven throughout the triangular logic of Chapter 1.

The exercise below that Don Seidel shared with me illustrates the point that what we provide students must have meaning to them – which is not always the case.

After a description/discussion of learning triangles I ask the group two questions...

"How many of you can speak Icelandic?"
"How many of you have been to Iceland?"

As you might surmise no one has said *yes* as yet. "Well then...today I'm going to teach you to pronounce a famous Icelandic term."

Usually blank stares exist at this point.

"I'm going to spell this term for you. You will then try
to correctly pronounce it with your partner. You are
welcome to write it down. Okay, listen carefully.
H - E - S - T - A - S - K - I - T - U - R
One more time.
H - E - S - T - A - S - K - I - T - U - R
Now give it a try."

Talk about the Tower of Babel. A cacophony of weird noises breaks out. Some credible, some humorous, almost all incorrect. After a few minutes, their attention is returned to the presenter. "Thank you. Who thinks they have it right and would like to share the saying with the group?" No one volunteers. The patience of the presenter prevails, and eventually one says the term.

"Heestaski-ter" says the first volunteer.
"No, nice try, how about another," prompts the presenter.
"His task is sure," says one who feels she has broken the code of the presenter's trickery.
"No not close...thanks, another."
Well after several other attempts, some close, some not, the presenter says...

"Let me help a bit..." and proceeds to show them some visual clues on the overhead projector.
Hest - as - key - tur.
"Now try sharing it with your partner again."

Invariably they come up with a close approximation of the term. As a few display their linguistic mastery of the term the rest join in the consensus of pronunciation. The presenter guides them through a series of choral demonstrations of their new learning mastery...

"HEST AS KEY TUR!"
"HEST AS KEY TUR!"

Individuals are chosen to show their individual accomplishment...

"Hest as key tur"
"Hest as key tur"

Again the group...

"HEST AS KEY TUR!"
"HEST AS KEY TUR!"
"How do you feel about it? How fine a job you've done!" extolls the presenter.

After a few minutes, inevitably one member of the group says. "What does it mean?" Silence fills the room and the presenter says. "In Icelandic, hestaskitur means the droppings of a horse!"

As you would expect everyone laughs heartily at this point. As the room returns to normal, the presenter says. "And I suggest that hestaskitur is precisely what we often give to our kids when we present our curriculum!"

Discussion with the group then centers on drawing meaning to our curriculum from the application of learning triangles. The assessment of 25 years of shadow studies, (Lounsbury & Clark, 1991) indicates that our curricula are artifically removed from the life and needs of our learners. The authors identify how our students passively parrot back information without understanding the meaning or applicability of their learning to the real world. Having students sit as passive "sponges" and spend their days in rigid schedules, grouped and thereby pigeon-holed by ability, and taught in a manner that dishes out massive doses of unrelated content is developmentally insensitive to the needs of our children.

The learning environment of the classroom should be revamped to give students an opportunity to participate, probe, and perform. Questioning, choosing options which they help determine, enables students to be engaged and responsible. Passivity is an element of the controlling environment while engaged learning is characteristic of an enabling environment.

The "hestaskitur" example encourages us to relate to what we often do to our students. The enabling environment breaks the paradigms of traditional practices and opens new possibilities of blending sound theoretical practice with the excitement of engaged involvement. It is incumbent on each of us to make an enlightened choice.

2. THE ENABLING ENVIRONMENT understands, appreciates, and validates the worth of students and staff. (Chapter 2)

The second chapter reviewed the factors that makes children, particularly adolescents, tick. Within our young people at this rapidly changing time of life the closest thing to human nuclear fusion on this planet occurs when *TESTOSTERONE MEETS ESTROGEN*!

While we may use humor in describing our youngsters, we know that how they feel about themselves and how people treat them when they are on the staging ground of their adulthood is no laughing matter.

It is not sufficient to only know what makes our kids tick. Understanding, while important, is secondary to what you do about it. The enabling environment recognizes that a nurturing attitude helps create productive, well adjusted children.

Knowledge begets action in the enabling environment. When photographs of students and staff decorate classroom walls, corridors, and even the entrances to the school itself, all get the impression that people count here. Of course photographs don't do it alone; pictures need to be backed up with consistent action as well. Let me illustrate.

Continuous development is an important element of life. As youngsters find out who they are and what they can become, they need to know that what they are experiencing is natural, right, and that they are not alone. An adolescent picture board is a way to display your understanding, appreciation, and validation of the students who attend your school.

A picture board is a way to display a school's positive view of its students.

In the foyer of our middle school, we display a 5' x 8' free standing picture board. On the burlap covered homosote surface are photographs of our students succeeding and applying themselves in academic, exploratory, co-curricular and social situations. Interactions with teachers, peers and the total learning program are visually depicted and prominently displayed. Also on that large picture board are sayings that portray to our youngsters and to our visitors what the compelling "world of adolescence" is all about.

We have gotten a great deal of mileage from the picture board. Though the display is important, the substance of the idea occurs when the administrators meet in team sessions with every new student to our school and present a motivational talk on adolescence. Understanding becomes action when administrators join staff in helping our students better understand the "essence of their adolescence."

When the students are told that the assistant principal was shaving when he was in eighth grade and the principal says it took him until his junior year in high school, kids get another indication that:

- People mature at different rates

- It's okay to do so

- Their two administrators are people too

- Their administrators matured at different rates

- It was okay for them to do so

- That their assistant principal was a wooly mammoth
  when he was in middle school.

There's no magic in the idea of a picture board or talking with kids about their development – just some sensitivity to our youngsters' development, a tad of creativity, and a willingness to take the time to make it possible.

———————●———————

3. THE ENABLING ENVIRONMENT has staff who are in touch with their motivators, needs, and professional patterns of interaction. (Chapter 3)

The third chapter reviewed the perfectionistic obsessiveness that occurs when people try to control all the variables of their lives. Control by limiting variables is the be-all and end-all for these types as they prefer order over relationships. By reducing the number of variables with which they have to contend, perfectionists mistakenly assume that they are in control.

The chapter reviewed the differentiation between perfectionism and high standards; the latter being a target that people could aim for and hit. For example, how many of us would accept the notion of a "drop rate" for obstretricians in delivering new born babies. You know we're all human, everybody makes mistakes – 15% dropped, 10%, 5%...of course not, we would only tolerate a 0% rate of drop.

In the enabling environment school how many failing students do we accept? 15% – 10% – 5%...we should only accept a 0% rate of failure and devote our energies to achieving that goal.

An example of perfectionism was used by TV personality Jennifer James (1985). She queries her audience...

"How many of you could sleep well at night knowing that a jar of maraschino cherries had spilled on your white formica table top? And how many of you could leave them there 'til morning?"

Almost all state that they'd get up to clean up the mess before they could close their eyes. James reinforces this point by further asking...

"Well if the kitchen isn't your thing, how many of you could rest easily if that same bottle of maraschino cherries were spilled all over the hood of your new car?"

Wrestle with those images if you will. Could you sleep if either one affected your property? I couldn't. Yet I know that in the enabling environment, were you to face sticky circumstances like the above, that you wouldn't have to face them alone (even though perfectionists tend to feel isolated).

Concern for doing a task well is not perfectionism. Doing well at something is just good business. Cleaning a spilled mess is logical. Controlling your environment may make you feel good; you seemingly are in charge, but this false sense of security denies the inevitability that life happens all around us. The jar of life spills its contents readily. Dealing with problems decisively rather than building up an aversion or letting problems fester, helps to determine our organizational effectiveness. How we view the world – how we perceive things around us – is crucial.

For example, think of the water glasses in a fancy hotel room. You go into the antiseptically clean environment. You feel good – even the water glasses are sterile. Aren't they wrapped in clear plastic? But think about it...who may have put the glasses in the plastic? Right...the person who just cleaned the commode!

The water glasses could conceivably be different than what they appear to be. So too is perfectionism. While perfectionism gives us a sense of control and order, understanding comes from an analysis of the patterns which we unconsciously follow; patterns which we need to periodically assess in order to define reality.

Burns (1987), conducted a study of a major insurance company's top 69 salespeople. He found that those who had perfectionistic tendencies, earned $8 to $10,000 less a year than those who did not. Studies consistently reaffirm that high performers are almost always free of the compulsion to be perfect. They concern themselves with the quality of the journey rather than the destination, and regard mistakes not as failures but as learning points (feedback) so they can do better the next time.

The enabling environment nurtures people who grow from taking risks, and who value children by treating student mistakes as instructional opportunities to further the learning of their youngsters.

The enabling environment establishes a secure yet challenging environment so people may leave the comfort zone of a safe harbor to test their assumptions and grow through trial, error, and feedback; to clean up the "spills" of life with confidence, collaboration, and competence.

———————●———————

4. THE ENABLING ENVIRONMENT collaboratively involves people in the process of change. (Chapter 4)

The process whereby one proactively faces windows of change was the focus of Chapter 4. The point was made there that if you plant a tree, don't keep pulling it up by the roots to check out how it is growing. CHANGE requires time, as do the people who are undergoing it.

Perspective is critically important as we change. Initially we might resist change, but when it has been successfully accomplished we look back and call it growth. One of the "safest" areas where change can be effectively implemented is in the physical environment of the school. People are visual. They notice differences; be it a hairstyle, new outfit, or the way one walks.

In moving toward the development of our middle school from the junior high that had been in existence for over twenty-five years, we concentrated on multiple fronts, one being the common environment of the school. Just as the teacher teaches, just as the principal teaches, just as the school secretary teaches, just as all teach, so too does the environment.

Recognizing this fact and blending visual, attitudinal and organizational **change** together, staff efforts resulted in the creation of our enabling environment. A few years later we received a prestigious award from the National School Public Relations Association for *catching people doing things right.*

Ours was not a casual approach to building aesthetics and student recognition. It was heavily measured and factored into our mission. The process began with staff meetings regularly addressing the topic "How can we improve the environment of our school?" A meeting was devoted to sharing ideas. Another featured an "internal field trip" in which staff could visit as many classrooms as time permitted to observe and note exciting ideas and visuals that were a part of each room's environment. A Principal's Advisory Council representing each discipline was selected to review new ideas. An annual staff questionnaire was developed in which, among other things, staff were asked to rate student recognition efforts at the Middle School and suggest or comment on ideas for recognition and building aesthetics.

Based on their input, specific plans for student recognition and building aesthetics were included in the school's annual objectives. A professional photographer was hired to take full face candid pictures and a new design for stationery and handbook covers that used students' pictures were developed.

Some staff and students with an award from the National School Public Relations Association for catching people doing things right.

The custodial staff built display cases and contributed other fix-up touches. Donated bookcases, display cases, shelves and other useful equipment were picked up from private individuals, store closings, and business surplus.

The school has been enhanced by a myriad of visuals. One display case headed, "These Visitors Think Our School Is Special," features visitors' letters and a map pinpointing where they've come from. A picture board highlights the pursuit of excellence through honors, attendance and visuals that say "You make a difference and count." Large pictures of students adorn the halls. A special banner welcomes students, staff and visitors. Hanging plants add warmth to glassed-in bridges. Displays of art work and writing complement concerts. Students, staff and guests can leave messages to one another on the "You're Special" board. Room numbers have been replaced by "at home and personal" pictures of faculty and staff from their family photo albums.

A state map highlights teams from visiting districts.

The students, staff, commmunity and administrators are very proud of our school...*and the enabling environment we all helped to create.* Collaboratively creating, we faced change in a proactive fashion. And where do we hang our certificate of recognition? Not in some office, but in the corridors for all to see.

William Heard Kilpatrick said...

"We learn what we live, and we learn it to the degree that we live it."

Learning to deal with change means to both live with and create it. Take a slow walk through your school and see how you might make it an even more enabling environment than it currently is.

---●---

5. THE ENABLING ENVIRONMENT periodically asks why are we doing what we're doing?...and utilizes past and present success as benchmarks for future accomplishments.
(Chapter 5)

Lounsbury (1990) reminds us that "the school is a teacher" and encourages us to consider specifically just what the school is teaching via its programs, policies, rules and regulations, by its way of life.

In the fifth chapter we did that, assessing, analyzing, and recommending a course of *action*. As the school is not just a physical place in which teachers conduct classes, it is an environment wherein youth grow, we must be highly conscious of its culture, remembering that the school is a "powerful teacher presenting its lessons silently but surely."

The activities at the end of Chapter 5 were designed to have the reader become more in touch with decisions and patterns of behavior that may be played out as a matter of course in the life of the school. These examples portrayed powerful negative implications for the culture of the school; especially if they were not challenged.

Lounsbury also suggests a series of questions for us to actively consider as we come to grips with the implicit curriculum.

• What is taught by the school's grading system? (As a result...) what do students readily conclude are the real objectives of our school? Does the grading system even sometimes teach students how to cheat?

• What lessons are inherent in our discipline codes and policies? Are they based on negative assumptions about the nature of early adolescents? Do they often encourage kids to learn ways to beat the system? Do students learn, regretably, the lesson that adults don't trust us?

• Does the school's modus operandi teach young people compliant behavior, even as we profess to be helping them develop their individuality and initiative?

Valuing others is a part of a positive environment.

• Though not our intention, isn't it likely that our tracking and ability grouping practices will teach young people that some are worth more than others? What sort of self-concept can be developed by those who spend all day in lower sections? (p. 41)

Some probing questions and a call to reflect on what we're doing. If in our enabling environment we periodically call "time" and then ask, why are we doing what we're doing? the school becomes the realistic arena where life is lived and progress in meeting the mission of the school is assured. Keep this thought in mind when we reflect on the case studies that follow.

———————————•———————————

6. THE ENABLING ENVIRONMENT empowers all in planning, reaching, and maintaining a synergized team. (Chapter 6)

The development of an enabling environment takes time, commitment, and sharing. One of the key elements of this sharing is effective communications, not just talking, but via many and *effective means of communication*. These communications lead to a more complete understanding of why decisions take place, support a give and take culture that operates on the higher levels of the communications mountain, and give all a share in the decision making process.

In the empowered organization each takes a role in communicating and deciding. In the enabling environment communications are linked so that the probability of making effective decisions increases. You may draw some inferences about these points from an analysis of three dramatically different but actual case studies.

Case Studies in Communications

Directions: Read each case study. Ask yourself if there is a potential problem. If so what do you do about it? If not, would you do anything with the information you've just read? Please try case study #1 before reading #2 and #2 before #3.

Case Study #1
     This journal entry was written by a student and given to the student's *English teacher*. You are that teacher and you are known for your ability to work with your students. What do you do?

What's It Worth?

*What's it worth when
you lose all your friends?*

*What's it worth when
you lose the ones you so
deeply cared for?*

*What's it worth when
you lose all confidence
you once had in yourself?*

*What's it worth when
you lose all hope?*

*Well my friend, these
are facts of life, and life
is not worth it!*

Is there a problem? What is it?

If so, what do you do about it?

If not, is there anything you'd like to do with the information?

Case Study #2

A multiple copy referral form written by the technology teacher on the behavior of an 8th grade student we will call Barbara reaches your desk. As the *building principal*, what do you do?

Teacher___R----------_____Date___3/15___
Student___Barbara---------_____Time___2:10 pm

Teacher Statement of Situation: Student has not
done anything all year. She floats
around the class disturbing other
students. I have assigned her to a
corner of the room where she will not
disturb anyone and bother people who
want to be here. I have had it.
Teacher Signature: _____

Action Taken by Teacher to Obtain Improvement_ I have
talked to her twice and have not gotten
results. I recommend that we remove
her from this class.

Is there a problem? What is it?

Is so, what do you do about it?

If not, is there anything you'd like to do with the information?

Case Study #3

The personal statement in this case study was given to a nurturing art teacher by one of her students. It was unsolicited. The art teacher hands it to you in the staff room and asks you what you think. As a *colleague*, what do you think, do and/or say?

I Am Me

In all the world, there's no one else exactly like me. Everything that comes out of me is authentically mine because I alone chose it. I own everything about me: my body, my feelings, my mouth, my voice, all my actions, whether they be to others or myself. I own my fantasies, my dreams, my hopes, my fears. I own all my triumphs and successes, all my failures and mistakes.

Because I own all of me, I can become intimately acquainted with me. By doing so I can love me and be friendly with me in all my parts. I know there are aspects about myself that puzzle me and others aspects that I do not know.

But as long as I am friendly and loving to myself I can courageously and hopefully look for solutions to the puzzles and for ways to find out more about me. However I look, sound, whatever I say and do and whatever I think and feel at a given moment in time is authentically me. If later some part of how I looked, sounded thought and felt turn over to be unfitting, I can discard that which is unfitting, keep the rest and invent something new for that which I discarded.

I can see, hear feel, think, say and do. I have the tools to survive, to be close to others, to be productive and to make sense and order out of the world of people and things outside of me. I own me and therefore I can engineer me.

I am me and I am okay.

Is there a problem? What is it?

If so, what do you do about it?

If not, is there anything you'd like to do with the information?

Discussion of Case Study #1...(You are the English teacher.)

You see a real problem here. Words like *depressed, conflicted*, and *suicidal* immediately come to mind. As people who attempt suicide often telegraph their inclination as many as twelve times prior to attempting it, this journal writing must be taken seriously. It is not something that you grade "C+" then move on to the next student's writing.

In responding you no doubt took a number of actions. Some probably included...

• Finding time to quietly speak with the student before the class period had ended.

• Listened to the student's feelings when you were able to talk.

• Spoke with the student's counselor and/or the school psychologist.

• Alerted your administrator to the possible problem.

• Shared the information with a colleague to ask for a verification of your interpretation.

You moved quickly and did not hold this information in overnight, or the weekend. Here is a student possibly in big time trouble. You were a resource and you sought professional assistance for the student.

Well done!

Discussion of Case Study #2...(You are the principal)

You may have had mixed feelings about this one. On the one hand you recognize the frustration on the part of the teacher – end of the day, distractible behavior by the non-engaged student, Tech class, possible hazard, and the like.

Yet you notice that here it is with approximately 6-1/2 months of the school year gone and the teacher has only "talked to the student." Assigning a student to a corner of the room may have been intended to isolate the behavior but it obviously hasn't worked – in fact it may have worsened the behavior. It's a poor management technique anyhow. The student has really pushed this teacher's "hot button."

As the principal you speculate whether this teacher was just blowing off steam, knowing that you'd never send this home to the parent, or whether on this day (The Ides of March) he finally did lose it. You've been in the class and know that the kid hasn't been a problem while you were there. So what do you do?

Though your inclination might be to give this colleague a free ticket to the local career counseling center, you know that this teacher is asking for help no matter how poorly presented was the written referral. You need more information and you speak to the teacher, careful to provide support, yet trying to get some objective data to better understand the nature of the problem. You talk with the counselor and some other colleagues and design a tentative course of action. It may be that you...

• Consider a third party counseling the student while you work on a classroom management plan with the teacher.

• Talk with the student and lay out your expectations for her classroom behavior...and/or discover why she's doing what she's doing.

• Suggest and/or join with the teacher in developing some positive actions, such as calling the parents to enlist their assistance, taking a look at student classroom jobs to see if Barbara can modify her approach by becoming more responsible, looking at the curriculum to see if the tasks are appropriate to the age level and/or Barbara's learning style, etc., etc., etc.

While the second case study does not have the immediacy of the first, there is definitely a need for action.

Discussion of Case Study #3... (You are the colleague of the nurturing art teacher who asked you for your reaction to this statement.)

What a difference from the other two! Now here is a secure kid – here's a student who at first blush has it all together. "I am me, and I am okay." Wouldn't it be nice if the others had that same sense of confidence and presence.

You congratulate this superb teacher for drawing out the talent of this youngster. You admire the student's advanced writing style and ask if this sharing was in some way related to a project that the teacher had used in the classroom. You wish you had the student in your class.

But as you walk away you begin to wonder if there wasn't something more that met the eye. The statement was vaguely familiar. Why did the student seek the approbation of her superb art teacher? Was the student's approval statement of being "okay" a facade masking a feeling of major doubt? If so, was this doubt the natural insecurity of adolescents or was it more? You hit the pillow that night vowing to revisit the topic tomorrow to extoll the virtues of the writer and the art teacher – but curious to know if there's more than you first thought.

———————●———————

A question to now ask is...If you could choose but one of these three very different students for your class (or school) which one would it be? You can only choose one...

...the poet
...the technology floater
...the self-esteemed art student

In workshops where these case studies are presented more often than not there is a healthy mix of those who select each student with a slightly higher inclination for the art student. Why did you choose the one you did? Are you comfortable with your choice?

The late Truman Capote in one of his books had a character who wrote his signature in three different handwritings. When asked why he did this, he, in essence, said..."I write as I am at any given time. And I am never quite the same." Our three dramatically different case studies are all of the same person! A fourteen-year-old eighth grade female foster child we call Barbara who had been abused as a young girl.

Barbara who...wrote in her journal her suicidal poem as a flag for her fine English teacher, *as a cry for help*. That teacher talked to the student immediately and within five minutes after English class had ended, she had shared the substance of the poem and the student's comments with me. Our psychologist had contact with the student shortly thereafter. The foster parent was involved later that day. Barbara's plea was real. She had attempted suicide before and was contemplating it again. We were able to help the student due to the actions taken by the teacher and support staff.

Barbara who...floated around the technology classroom disturbing others, causing the teacher to exclaim, "I have had it." Barbara had been a problem; she was not engaged in this hands-on class program – which by most standards was a very good one. She had a history of reacting poorly to male teachers, didn't like kinesthetic learning and was easily distractible. When made fully aware of Barbara's circumstances, the teacher gave her more directed learning rather than choice activities, and worked with Barbara's counselor to build a bridge to a more positive instructional relationship. Consequently, Barbara was able to "make it" through the technology sequence in good shape.

Barbara who...gave her statement of personal worth to her nurturing art teacher. Barbara wanted so desperately to be valued by this master teacher...this creative, talented human being...that she copied Virginia Satir's powerful *I am Me* and tried to pass it off as her own work. When this happened the teacher shared the work with her colleagues, in order to validate her own professional impressions of this student. This teacher had succeeded with Barbara as none of her colleagues had; yet she sought others' opinions as a means of helping her to design a plan to increase Barbara's success.

And where is Barbara today? She's functioning well. Against the predictions of some, she has graduated from high school, has a job and has even taken some art courses at the local community college.

What does Barbara's story tell us?

In my judgment we all need to be in touch with the many faces of the "Barbaras" in our classrooms, schools, and organizations. When the English teacher identified a problem she immediately sought the counsel of her colleagues; colleagues whom she respected, to marshall assistance for a needful student, at a crucial crossroads in the youngster's life.

A teacher who needed the assistance reached out to an administrative colleague, who didn't reject the teacher's cry for help when he needed to get a different slant on how to help a student in his technology class.

And Barbara's story tells us that no matter how talented; or how effective we may be as a professional in working with a student, that we all need one another's perspective to become even more effective. When this process occurs as a result of "the way we do things around here," you can reach an uncommon level of success in your learning environment.

Teachers who discuss students in teams are more effective in helping their students.

A synergized team operating in an enabling environment will encourage the Barbaras of your school to become more successful than the inhibiting circumstances that their background might suggest. Each adult had strength in the formula that enabled Barbara to grow. Seek the development of your team – and draw from the rich talent and perspectives of all. As in T. E. A. M.,

TOGETHER EVERYONE ACHIEVES MORE!

7. THE ENABLING ENVIRONMENT recognizes that shared leadership increases ownership for decision making and organizational productivity. (Chapter 7)

CROCK BILL RECHIN AND DON WILDER

Reprinted with special permission of King Features Syndicate, Inc.

The speed of the leader determines the rate of the pack, some say. In Chapter 7 we argued that a swiftly moving pack with ownership and responsibility for the organization increases the effectiveness of the leadership as well as that of the organization itself. Building on the synergized team concept in the sixth chapter, our review of leadership/shared decision making, defined the interdependence that comes when all are empowered. The enabling environment facilitates that connectedness.

Among the elements of effective leadership were *humor, perspective* and *timing*. Leadership also must be clear and responsive to the objectives of the organization.

Clarity is essential as demonstrated in this familiar anecdote.

A governmental bureaucrat received a letter from a person who wanted to know whether he could use hydrocloric acid to clean the tubes of his steam boiler. The official wrote back...

Uncertainties of reactive processes make the use of hydrocloric acid highly undesirable where alkalinity is involved.

To which the man wrote...

Thanks for the advice. I'll start using it next week.

The bureaucrat wired back this urgent message...

Regrettable decision involves many uncertainties. Hydrocloric acid will incur sublimate invalidating reactions.

Which elicited this response from the grateful citizen...
Thanks again. Glad to know its okay.

This time an urgent but clear message was sent...

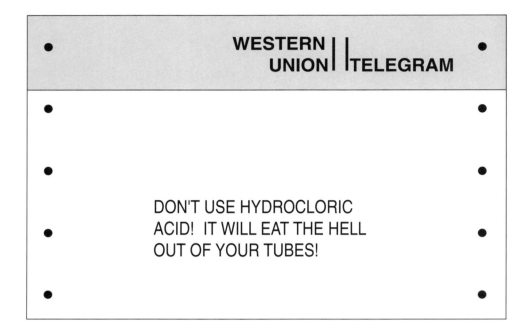

Leaders, don't fall over your words. Simple, clear direct communications work best.

Some consistently evident truths become apparent when interacting with administrators. The great majority of designated leaders are hard working, have fine people skills, and are talented. And although most are sincere and humble, a sizeable number have an aggrandized sense of their importance, which outstrips the talents that others believe they have. In other words the Coperni-can view of the center of the universe being the sun is not shared by these few individuals – they are the center of all that is worthy! To these individuals (and in a sense to all who lead) we dedicate this 17th Century Prayer...

LORD Thou knowest better than I know myself that I am growing older and will some day be old. Keep me from the fatal habit of thinking I must say something on every subject and on every occasion. Release me from craving to straighten out everybody's affairs. Make me thoughtful but not moody; helpful but not bossy. With my vast store of wisdom, it seems a pity not to use it all, but Thou knowest Lord that I want a few friends at the end.

Keep my mind free from the recital of endless details; give me wings to get to the point. Seal my lips on my aches and pains. They are increasing, and love of rehearsing them is becoming sweeter as the years go by. I dare not ask for grace enough to enjoy the tales of others' pains, but help me to endure them with patience.

I dare not ask for improved memory, but for a growing humility and a lessing cocksureness when my memory seems to clash with the memories of others. Teach me the glorious lesson that occasionally I may be mistaken.

Keep me reasonably sweet; I do not want to be a Saint — some of them are so hard to live with — but a sour old person is one of the crowning works of the devil. Give me the ability to see good things in unexpected places, and talents in unexpected people. And, give me, O Lord, the grace to tell them so.

17th Century Prayer

The enabling environment encourages this *perspective*, and looks beyond the personal foibles of those who may be unduly "taken by themselves." The environment enables those few to contribute as well. When leaders blend with the group so that their skills magnify the talents of others, then synergy really happens. **Power shared empowers all!**

Leaders also need to have a keen sense of timing...as Dik Browne's Hagar once again illustrates.

Reprinted with special permission of King Features Syndicate, Inc.

Leadership is fostered in the enabling environment. Leadership is the concern of all – and all demonstrate leadership. Teachers are leaders and administrators are leaders of leaders. If you live this attitude, very special sparks of collaboration will be ignited especially as you fulfill your organizational potential with humor and a smile.

8. THE ENABLING ENVIRONMENT is philosophically, visually, procedurally, and aesthetically congruent with the purposes of the organization. (Chapter 8)

To this point we've set the puzzle pieces of the empowered school into the backdrop of an enabling environment. We've looked at the fit of theory – our students, ourselves, change, the three "A's" of assessment/analysis/action, teamwork, and leadership. We found that these elements fall into place when the setting is right. And we found that the setting is both physical and attitudinal.

The last piece in completing the jigsaw of any enabling environment is one that you can have a great deal of fun with. It is tangible. Everyone can achieve it. And when done well it can establish a momentum that will spread like wildfire in your empowered organization.

The visual dimension of the empowered school is that "it" – tangible symbols that "people matter here." It is the clearly laid out incentives to which our students may aspire. The *aesthetics emphasis* of the middle school is an effective way to demonstrate that the school environment is also a powerful teacher.

Despite the importance of the setting and symbols, the visual environment is not generally recognized for the dynamic element that it is. Consider what the U. S. Office of Education looks for when evaluating schools in its Secondary School Recognition Program:

- Clear educational goals
- High expectations for students
- Order, discipline and freedom from drug use
- Rewards and incentives for students
- Rewards and incentives for teachers (notice...no mention of "staff" which is a more inclusive term)
- Regular and frequent monitoring of student progress
- Development of good character and values
- Concentration on academic learning time
- Positive school climate
- Administrative leadership
- Well articulated curricula
- Parent and community support and involvement

Other than raising some semantic arguments, nearly everyone would agree with the importance of these points. Yet there is a prominent omission – there was no mention of the *enabling environment*. (Keep in mind that climate is not the environment. Climate is how you feel about the *culture* of the school.) To correct that omission a few stories and pictures follow.

When the new principal came to Churchville-Chili junior high several years ago, he recognized that though a good school, the environment of this 500 pupil organization was sterile. He had brought with him a beautiful banner from his former school. The banner had been hung outside the main office and served as a symbol of that school's priorities. It extended a warm welcome to visitors.

It was an 8' x 4' hand-sewn banner replete with a sun and lettering welcoming people to the school. It was special and when installed at CCJHS, would herald a new visual sense of welcome to an otherwise pretty sterile place. The principal approached the Director of Building and Grounds, a hard working non-risk taking colleague to share his idea.

"Oh, we don't do things like that around here," said Bruce.

"Well, why not?" said the newcomer.

"The kids would tear it down in a day!"

The principal said..."Bruce, I can appreciate that you haven't done things like this before. But I'm so absolutely certain that everyone will respect this banner, that I'll buy you a fine steak dinner in the restaurant of your choice if the kids harm this banner in any way!"

"I can taste it now!" said Bruce.

Up it went...and eight years later there it stays--as yet without a single mark on it. It has provided a back drop for photographs with lunar astronauts – introductory shots for television and newspaper features on the school a sense of welcome for all – and a chance to capture a few characters on film along the way.

This picture of John Barnard and his strong friend indicates that in an empowered school people support one another (particularly our students) along the way. (Actually John's supportive friend was a clever halloween costume he wore at a student council dance.) Visually you get a glimpse of the banner and some student art work on display.

"Round two" with Bruce came when after talking with a new art teacher who was excited about displaying the projects of her students in the corridor, the principal spoke once again to the Director of Buildings and Grounds. "Bruce, we're anxious to display the talents of our students this fall. What do you say to..."

"I don't have any money. What's this going to cost?"

"Almost nothing for me – absolutely nothing for you," said the principal as he continued his previous thought. "In fact, a very inexpensive way is to install a long wire anchored to the wall and we can display a great deal of art work on it by using opened paper clips as hangars."

"The kids are going to destroy them."

"Name the restaurant, Bruce!"

"I can taste it now," said Bruce.

We have now displayed the surprising art talent of our students for eight plus years. Over seven thousand pieces of art have been hung in the corridor galleries of the school. Not one picture, one graphic, or one print has been touched.

Students proudly display their art projects.

Later during that first season of our school's metamorphosis, a tremendous idea surfaced during a staff meeting. During a brainstorming session in which the staff met in small sub-groups to wrestle with the question, "What can be done to make our school environment even more special?", one teacher came up with an idea he had harbored for years. The bridges connecting the wings of our school with all their glass surfaces were natural greenhouses. Why not install hanging baskets with plants for all to enjoy? Great idea!

I don't have to share what Bruce's reaction was to this one...suffice to say he's still waiting for dinner. In fact, the students water and care for the plants to this day.

This doesn't mean that this idea hasn't at times presented a problem for us. Red spider mites got into the plants on the back bridge a few years ago in April. It decimated the plant stock. Unbeknownst to the rest of us, a staff member took cuttings from the front bridge and grew them to healthy full sized plants. Late one Friday afternoon in September she came in and made the back bridge green again! That happens in organizations where ownership and pride are shared.

Meanwhile ideas proliferated both in and out of the classroom setting. Each office space and classroom now has a plexiglass plate on the wall near the corridor door displaying a picture of the person who "owns" that space. Pictures of one's family, a trip to the zoo, a philosophic touchstone which the staff member enjoys, etc., bid welcome and the sense that *people matter here*. Though a few staff are camera shy and just have their name artistically printed outside the door, here are examples of what a few of the name plates look like.

Social Studies Teacher, John DeBaun

Secretary and Alternative Classroom Supervisor, Sue Call

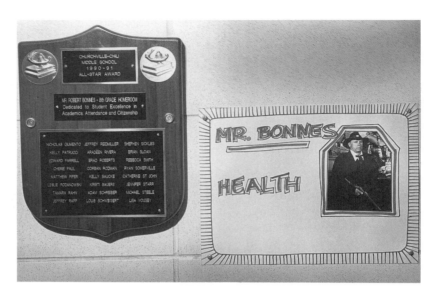

Health Teacher, Bob Bonnes (also shown is the All-Star Plaque for Bob's homeroom students who were the lead group in academics, attendance and citizenship for the grade that year)

What of Bruce during all this CHANGE?

He was tremendously supportive.

Custodial staff members were instrumental in building large display bulletin boards. Bruce's leadership was fantastic.

Cost-effective display projects may be built in-house.

Custodians Maryanne Young and John Palmer showing off John's handiwork which contain a three-year historical log of photographs of the 6th, 7th and 8th grade students.

Meanwhile, Bruce squeezed blood from a stone and found funds from his hard-pressed budget to advance the aesthetic display of the school. The rear wall of the cafeteria was replaced by burlap covered homosote for the display of student work. Bruce had not only become a believer, but a leader in implementing positive change.

Meanwhile explosions of a similar nature were occurring in each classroom. Those who had previously "dressed up" their instructional space continued to do so. Those who hadn't found encouragement from the examples that were set by colleagues and support from their leaders. They began to change their classrooms as well. The culture of the school had changed to enable the classrooms to be more vibrant and more in line with the mission of the school. In-building "field trips" highlighting the room environments were taken. Ideas were shared and the pattern of isolation (Chapter 1) became a distant memory.

Support staff using the reading loft in their skills center.

We soon learned that when students had expectations clearly established for them and when they knew their positive behaviors would be highlighted, that the kids responded in ways that were synchronous with the purposes of the school. Student behavior, scholarship, and cooperation improved because both the staff and the culture of the school modeled it.

Students reach for success when their accomplishments are highlighted.

We found that when the environment in the common areas of the school accented postives, individual classrooms soon followed suit. When individual staff members committed to a plan of action, then teams of teachers and departments did so as well. Prominently displaying student and staff accomplishments occurred throughout the building. A foxfire of positive energy ignited!

Thoughts about the classroom as an enabling environment came into clearer perspective. We found that the personality of a classroom is discernible; it has a character, a flavor all its own, and is a reflection of the teacher who inhabits it. **Difference** was interpreted as strength. As with the enabling environment of the school, the best classrooms were found to be purposeful, and in and of themselves served as powerful teachers. Consequently in assessing an individual classroom, you are encouraged to consider the following nine elements.

• **Motivation**. What does the teacher do to visually encourage students to risk, perform, and/or accomplish learning objectives?

The students and classroom of Colleen Currie.

- **Rewards**. Are there observable rewards or incentives on display?

- **Expectations**. Do students know what is expected of them and how are these expectations visually reinforced?

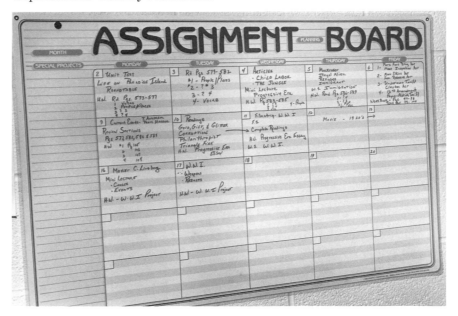

- **Color/Vitality**. Is the room alive, inviting and cheerful?

The science classroom of Fran Parnell

- **Curricular Display**. How are aspects of the curriculum displayed?

Robert Lupisella and his sixth grade students.

- **Student Recognition**. How are aspects of student success modeled? Are photographs of students and/or student work on display?

Several of the Grand National Champions of Quantum Magazine's Challenge for Excellence.

- **Uniqueness**. What makes this room unique?

- **Seating/Room Arrangement**. Does the room organization encourage interaction?

- **Humor**. How is humor used and for what purpose?

Pat Olson and Diane Boni welcome students to their "witching" classroom for a lesson on myths and mystery.

Motivation, rewards, expectations, color/vitality, curricular display, student recognition, uniqueness, seating/room arrangement, humor – all integrated to blend into an enabling classroom environment.

When you look at the aesthetic emphasis of our school you will note that our accomplishments are not magical. Talented? Perhaps. Creative? Most definitely. Special? Absolutely! Magical? No! Our plan was and is **achievable, attainable, and reachable**. Our uniqueness lies in the fact that we have consciously sought to engage everyone in the development of an enabling environment.

*The ultimate goal of the enabling environment is to support
a strong learning program.*

Along the way Churchville-Chili Middle School has been rewarded by the successes of our students, staff, and community. And when my esteemed colleague, Bruce, retired in 1990 still waiting for his steak dinner, he possessed an undeniable pride in what we all had created – together.

When people believe in their abilities and have the support and bites of success along the way, then the enabling environment becomes a reality. It begins with the commitment of one or a few. Their success when effectively modeled and encouraged by credible leaders becomes an organizational pattern. And that pattern returns the investment a hundred fold.

"The state of the facilities affects the way children learn. It's important to keep things nice."
**Bruce Erbelding
Superintendent of
Buildings and grounds
from 1960 to 1990**

The enabling environment that evolves in your setting may be dramatically different from the one at Churchville-Chili but the positive effects will be comparable. The vision begins with a commitment to action and the conscious choices of people who desire to make a difference.

Bruce did – and so can you!

End Notes

In each preceeding chapter some wisdom, a sprinkling of wit, and a strong sense of challenge were mixed in a blender. A wide variety of themes, concepts, and ideas were offered for consideration. Many were illustrated by examples, touchstones, diagrams, and the brush and pen of masterful philosophers who dwell beneath the mantel of the cartoons they draw.

If you have "stayed the course" then this smorgasbord of ideas and words has been of interest to you. Yet the validity of the written word lies not in its expression – but in its application. As an author I know that no matter how idealistic my design for your awareness may be that words are slippery, elusive things that do not lend themselves to machine like precision. Alfred North Whitehead, the great mathematician/philosopher, insisted that objective truths cannot be expressed in verbal terms.

Yet reading, as opposed to the "attention inertia" of watching television, enables us to become engrossed in puzzles. There is pleasure in incorporating a new insight into our lives, a delight in mastering new information and a challenge in playing with an author's words and ideas.

I hope my choice of words has communicated for you the topics related to an empowered organization. Each reader has to come to grips with the ideas presented in this work – to sift, sort, and perhaps choose to add them to one's personal agenda.

I wish you well with your choices for in choosing well we may better understand the foundations of instruction and communication. We may better understand ourselves – particularly our motivators and inhibitors. We will better understand our students and how to increase our positive influence on their lives. If we understand these dynamics then we can increase teamwork, leadership, and organizational harmony in getting to the core of our empowered schools. 🍎

REFERENCES

Allers, Robert D. (1982) "Children From Single-Parent Homes." *Today's Education*, Vol. 71 #3, pp. 68-70.

Arbuckle, Margaret and Lynn Murray. (1989) *Building Systems for Professional Growth*. Presque Isle, Maine: Maine State Department of Educational and Cultural Services.

Balguy, John. (1976) *The Foundation of Moral Goodness*. Reprint of the 1728-29 editions printed for J. Pemberton, London. New York: Garland Publishers.

Barker, Joel Arthur. (1988) *Discovering the Future (The Business of Paradigms)*. 2nd ed. Videotape. Minneapolis, Minnesota: Charthouse Learning Corporation.

Boike, Dennis. (1992) *Building Blocks of Self-Esteem*. Personal discussion with author.

Burns, David D. (1989) *The Feeling Good Handbook: Using the New Mood Therapy in Everyday Life*. New York: William Morrow & Company, Inc.

Buzan, Anthony. (1983) *Use Both Sides of Your Brain*. New York: E.P. Dutton.

Canfield, John and J. Wells. (1976) *100 Ways to Enhance Self-Concept in the Classroom*. Englewood Cliffs, New Jersey: Prentice-Hall.

Cassel, Pearl. (1980) *Lecture.* Toronto, Canada.

Cummings, Carol. (1983) *Managing to Teach*. Snohomish, Washington: Snohomish Publishing Company.

Dale, Edgar. (1972) *Building a Learning Environment*. Bloomington, Indiana: Phi Delta Kappa Educational Foundation.

Dobson, James. (First Quarter 1980) "The Agonies of Adolescence." *Life and Health Quarterly*, pp. 32-35.

Dreikurs, Rudolf and Pearl Cassel. (1972) *Discipline Without Tears*. New York: Hawthorne Books.

Elkind, David. (1988) *The Hurried Child: Growing Up Too Fast Too Soon*. Reading, Massachusetts: Addison-Wesley.

Erikson, Erik H. (1968) *Identity: Youth and Crisis*. New York: Norton Press.

Fulghum, Robert. (Fall/Winter 1990) "A Bag of Possibles and Other Matters of the Mind." *Newsweek*, Special Issue, pp. 88-92.

Garvin, James. (1989) *Learning How to Kiss a Frog.* Topsfield, Massachusetts: New England League of Middle Schools.

Gibran, Kahlil. (1973) *The Prophet.* New York: Knopf.

Hodgkinson, Harold. (1985) *Fearless Forecasts.* Personal discussion with author.

James, Jennifer. (1985) *Directions for Change: Excellence and Optimism.* Audio-tape. Seattle, Washington.

Johansen, Donald. (1976) "Tell Me What You Do." *NASSP Bulletin*, Vol. 60, pp. 63-65.

Johnson, David W. and Roger Johnson. (1984) *Cooperation in the Classroom.* Edina, Minnesota: Interaction Book Company.

Johnston, J. Howard. (1991) "How Do You Know That It Works?" in *Middle Level Education: Policies, Programs and Practices.* Edited by Capelluti and Stokes. Reston, Virginia: National Association of Secondary School Principals.

Joyce, Sean. (1985) *The Management Workshop.* New York: Dunn and Bradstreet.

Kirkpatrick, N.E. (1952) "The Mental Hygiene of Adolescents in Anglo-American Culture." *Mental Hygiene,* 36, pp. 394-403.

Kotter, John P. and Leonard Schlesinger. (March/April 1979) "Choosing Strategies for Change." *Harvard Business Review*, Vol. 57 #2, pp. 106-114.

LeBoeuf, Michael. (1985) *Greatest Management Principle in the World.* New York: Putnam Publishing Group.

Lounsbury, John and Donald C. Clark. (1990) *Inside Grade Eight: From Apathy to Excitement.* Reston, Virginia: National Association of Secondary Principals.

Lounsbury, John. (1991) "The Middel School Curriculum – Or is it Curricula?" in *Middle Level Education: Policies, Programs and Practices.* Edited by Capelluti and Stokes. Reston, Virginia: National Association of Secondary School Principals.

Lounsbury, John. (January 1990) "The School As Teacher." *Middle School Journal,* p 41.

Maslow, Abraham. (1970) *Motivation and Personality.* 2nd ed. New York: Harper and Row.

Nelson, Katheryn E. (1979) Talk given at the National Leadership Conference of the Association for Supervision and Curriculum Development, Washington D.C., 1979.

Osgood, William. (1980) *Basics of Successful Business Planning.* New York: Amacon.

Purkey, William. (1978) *Inviting School Success: A Self-Concept Approach to Teaching and Learning.* Belmont, California: Wadsworth Publishing.

Saphier, Jon and Matthew King. (March 1985) "Good Seeds Grow in Strong Cultures." *Educational Leadership,* pp. 67-74.

Schaefer, Charles E. (1979) *How to Influence Children.* New York: Van Nostrand Reinhold Publishers.

Scharenbroich, Mark. (1988) *The Greatest Days of Your Life...so far.* Film. Minneapolis, Minnesota: Jostens.

Schlecty, Phillip. (1990) *Schools for the 21st Century: Leadership Imperatives for Educational Reform.* San Francisco: Jossey-Bass Publishers.

Sizer, Theodore. (1984) *Horace's Compromise: The Dilemma of the American High School.* Boston: Houghton-Mifflin.

Slavin, Robert E. (1983) *Cooperative Learning.* New York: Longman Publishing Group.

Udall, Morris. (1988) *Too Funny to be President.* New York: Holt and Company.

von Oech, Roger. (1986) *A Kick in the Seat of Your Pants: Using Your Explorer, Artist, Judge and Warrior to be More Creative.* New York: Perennial Library.

Waitley, Denis. (1984) *The Psychology of Winning.* New York: Berkley Publishers.

Werge, Thomas. (Winter 90/91) "Did You Hear the One About...?" *Notre Dame Magazine,* Vol. 19 #4, pp. 16-22.

Wilkerson, William E. (1965) *Proceedings: Symposium on Congestion Theory.* Chapel Hill: University of North Carolina Press.

Wolfe, W. Beran. (1933) *Calm Your Nerves: The Prevention and Cure of Nervous Breakdown.* New York: Farrar & Rinehart.

About The Author

JOSEPH W. HOFF is presently the principal of an award winning middle school in Western New York State. Blending wit, current research, and practical how-to techniques, Dr. Hoff is a sought after keynote speaker and workshop presenter for regional, state, and national conferences. He has trained educators from fifty states and twenty foreign countries. Dr. Hoff's educational service includes teaching at both the elementary and secondary levels and principalships in elementary, middle, junior high, and high schools. He has coordinated districtwide staff development and personnel programs, and teaches graduate level courses on team-building, creating empowered schools, and middle grades issues in the Rochester, New York region. A frequent contributor to educational journals, this is his first book.